TRAVELS IN SEARCH OF
ENDANGERED SPECIES

TRAVELS IN SEARCH OF ENDANGERED SPECIES

JEREMY MALLINSON

FOREWORD BY GERALD DURRELL

Inscribed by the author
for Mike and Vibe
on the occasion of your
Silver Wedding Anniversary
With all best wishes
& love from

Pongo (alias Jeremy Mallinson!)

19th Jan. 1992.

DAVID & CHARLES
Newton Abbot London

For brother Miles, in celebration of all the fun
that we have shared together.

By the same author

Okavango Adventure
Earning your Living with Animals
Modern Classic Animal Stories (Editor)
The Shadow of Extinction
The Facts About a Zoo

Photographs are from the author's collection
unless stated otherwise

(Page 2) The golden-headed lion tamarin
(Jessie Cohen, NZP Smithsonian)

British Library Cataloguing in Publication Data

Mallinson, Jeremy
    Travels in search of endangered species
    1. Animals in danger of extinction
    I. Title
    591′.042

    ISBN 0–7153–9346–4

Phototypeset by ABM Typographics Ltd.
and printed in Portugal by Resopal
for David & Charles Publishers plc
Brunel House   Newton Abbot   Devon

Distributed in the United States by
Sterling Publishing Co, Inc,
2 Park Avenue, New York, NY 10016

Contents

The cultivation of
understanding and
mutual respect between
man and animal creates
a relationship which,
once achieved, is almost
impossible to surpass
(Robert Rattner)

Foreword

THERE are many different sorts of travel writers. Some are so dull, you wonder why they left home. Some weigh you down with a mass of unwieldy facts so that their book reads more like a museum catalogue than anything else. Others are so busy being sprightly and amusing that they leave you in some doubt as to whether or not they spent more than a hurried weekend at their destination. But among these extremes you can sometimes find a writer who is humorous, self-deprecating and informative. Jeremy Mallinson is one of these rare beasts, as rare as the beasts he describes so eloquently.

It is very rare for the charm, personality and dedication of an author to be reflected in his writing. In this book it shines out from every page and you are left feeling that not only have you met an extremely nice person but you have enjoyed their adventures with them. Wherever he goes, Jeremy leaves a host of admirers behind him, as I for one know, for I have followed in his footsteps, and would that all of us conservation travellers could say the same about our journeyings.

This is a book that is informative without finger-wagging, funny without being coy and a great pleasure to read. Jeremy has devoted his life to animals and they have repaid his devotion a hundredfold, as this book shows. It is a book that should be high on the list of every armchair traveller.

GERALD DURRELL

Introduction

WHEREAS Gerald Durrell had been smitten by what he referred to as 'zoomania' at the tender age of two and by the time he was six he had already set his sights on having a zoo of his own, by comparison I was a late convert to recognising the real significance of the role of a modern zoo with regard to conservation, education and research. In the spring of 1959, what began as little more than a temporary summer's employment at the newly founded Jersey Zoological Park, was soon to become my lifetime career and dedication. What I had not bargained for was that I would fall under Gerald Durrell's charismatic spell and at the same time come to appreciate the creative vision behind what he was soon to establish – the Jersey Wildlife Preservation Trust.

For as long as I can remember, I have been fascinated by anything to do with the animal kingdom, as well as to the quality of the natural world around me. Although no previous member of my family had any great concern for wildlife, I had been fortunate for, during the bleakest part of World War II, my parents had decided to send my elder brother, Miles, and myself to the safety of a preparatory school that was tucked amid the fells of the Lake District. A country mansion played host to the school, which was surrounded by a few hundred acres of wood and parkland, which in turn acted as a sanctuary to a wealth of animal life.

After the war the school moved to an even more spacious setting, near to Hadrian's Wall in Northumberland, where I continued observing wildlife. It was here that I was able to rejoice in having ready access to such an abundance of the animal kingdom to study, and, whenever possible, I would escape from the academic curriculum in order to ride unfettered, exploring every nook and cranny of the 1,500 acre country estate. These early exposures to such a diversity of animal life and unspoilt landscape sowed so many seeds of awareness that I have celebrated in having experienced and benefited from them ever since.

The final part of my twelve years at a boarding school was spent within the precincts of one of England's greatest cathedrals. Although my freedom had been curtailed by the harness of some eight hundred years of tradition, I developed a seemingly unquenchable thirst for reading as many travel books by great explorers, hunters and scientists that I could obtain. By the time I left that respectable place of learning and became a trainee in my father's wine and spirit firm in Jersey, I was already possessed with the ambition to travel to some of the continents and countries I had read about and in particular, to witness as much as possible of the natural world and the exotic animals that share the planet with us.

After just over a year as a vintner in Jersey, and somewhat fascinated by the travel experiences of such great African explorers as David Livingstone, Samuel

The Patron of the Jersey Wildlife Preservation Trust, The Princess Royal, shares a light-hearted moment with Gerald Durrell and the author (Jersey Evening Post)

9

Baker, Richard Burton, John Speke and Henry Morton Stanley, I signed on for a three-year term as a regular soldier to serve with the Rhodesia and Nyasaland Staff Corps, in the new federation's Central African Command. As my chief objective in travelling to Africa was to see as much of the continent and its wildlife as possible, I was fortunate in having picked a time of peace and prosperity, and the corps acted as an ideal host, enabling me to realise so many of my more adventurous goals, as well as to satisfy my ambition to see first-hand the diversity of Central Africa's animal kingdom.

During these first years in Africa I travelled extensively throughout Southern and Northern Rhodesia, Nyasaland to the Belgian Congo, within the Bechuanaland Protectorate and through South Africa. The more I witnessed the problems to which wildlife populations were increasingly being subjected, the more I realised that many of the various species of wildlife would ultimately be brought to the brink of extinction.

My next ambition was to join a government game department, but because of the Africanisation of so many of the jobs connected with wildlife, no worthwhile offers were forthcoming. I therefore decided to resign from the army and return to my Jersey home in order to reflect on what other careers might be open to me that could at least accommodate a modicom of my basic requirements to be directly involved with animals. The family wine and spirit business again opened its portals to me, and such other careers as the Hong Kong Police and tea planting in Assam similarly offered some future degree of financial security. However, as my thoughts crystallised I knew that somehow, on whatever terms, I needed to be working with animals. Whether they were domesticated or wild, in one way or another there simply had to be animals at the centre of my life.

As my destiny evolved, I embarked on a year of practical work on a dairy farm, which was at that time mandatory prior to gaining access to an agricultural college. A winter looking after seventy-six short-horn cattle in a well-mechanised farm situated among the hilliest region of Dorset failed to provide me with what I was seeking as my vocation in life.

A three-month kennel management course in the heart of Surrey's more prosperous commuter belt proved, through the diversity of the canines and felines I encountered, to be much more to my liking. When the course came to an end, I returned to Jersey with every intention of establishing my own kennels, for I planned to breed dogs of every kind for the connoisseur and hopefully to keep as many as possible to become my companions. My search for an appropriate property to convert was handicapped by both financial and planning restrictions. Because of various delays and frustrations experienced at this time, I applied for a temporary job at the recently opened Jersey Zoo. Such a decision had in no way been prompted by the fact that in those days I had been interested in zoos, but rather because I had just read Gerald Durrell's *My Family and Other Animals* and had been totally captivated by its contents.

Before long I was totally enamoured with the nature of my exotic wards and the temporary summer job of 1959 soon slid into the winter months while I worked as a member of the keepering staff, first involving myself with a wide variety of tropical birds and then venturing onto the mammal section to work with gorillas, marmosets, tapirs and peccaries – to mention only a few. So, at the age of twenty-three, I had finally found the degree of job satisfaction I had sought for such a long

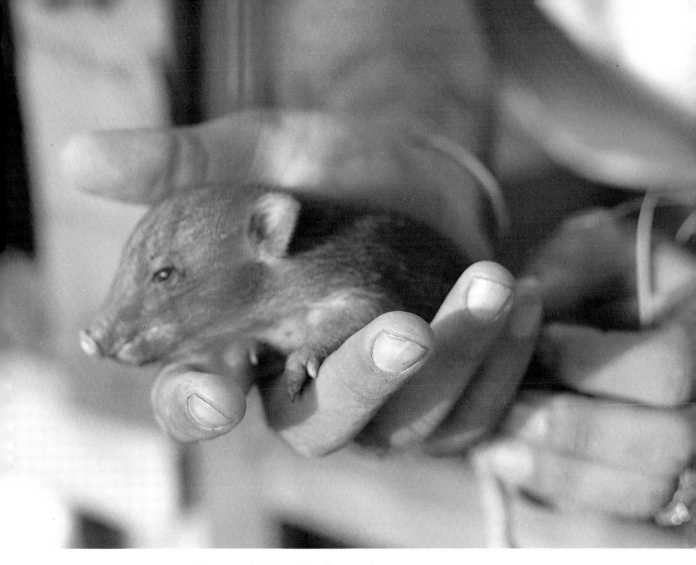

period. The zoo was in its infancy and although still struggling to survive, I was in mutual agreement with all of Gerald Durrell's ambitions for its future.

As my knowledge on the maintenance and breeding of exotic species began to grow, I gradually accumulated an impressive library of natural history books, over which I spent many hours of my free time. There was so much to learn and I came to regret that I had not had more formal training and undertaken a university zoology degree. However, I now recognised that I had a great deal of catching up to do and decided it would be beneficial to take leave of absence from the Jersey Zoo and to return to Africa.

The contents of my first book *Okavango Adventure* well covers my seven months in search of animals in southern Africa, during the period October 1961 to May 1962. During my animal collecting activities in both Southern Rhodesia (Zimbabwe) and Bechuanaland Protectorate (Botswana), I learnt a great deal from both my mistakes and successes, and it was fortunate that, after satisfying some of my desire to see Africa again, I rejoined the ranks of the Jersey Zoo animal staff and was promoted to the position of Gerald Durrell's deputy in the spring of 1963.

Looking back over my involvement with animals, I appreciate that I have been extremely fortunate in the way my enthusiasm for animal welfare and conservation has brought me into contact with so many delightful and dedicated

The pigmy hog represents, one of the world's rarest mammals due to the systematic loss of the majority of its remaining habitat, its last stronghold is the Manas Wildlife Sanctuary in Assam (Christian Schmidt)

11

The enforced introduction of domestic animals to exotic species does not always meet with success or is appreciated by all parties to the encounter (British Travel Association)

people. Paramount to this, of course, I well recognise how particularly lucky I was to meet Gerald Durrell at the time he launched his 'stationary ark', and, during the last thirty years, it has been my privilege to help with the development of the meaningful conservation work of the Wildlife Preservation Trusts, both in Jersey and overseas. Such good fortune has resulted in me fully concurring with the prophetic writings of Sir Nöel Coward, at one time an International Trustee of our Jersey Trust, when the 'master' hypothesised that, 'Work is so much more fun than fun!'

INTRODUCTION

During my extensive travels and field studies, as well as during my participation at many national and international conferences connected with various aspects of the future of wildlife, in particular with species conservation, I have come to recognise the importance for conservationists to adopt a far more inter-disciplinary approach so that we may maintain the degree of biological diversity that will hopefully provide future generations with the type of quality of life that we should like them to inherit.

Having drawn heavily from my extensive travel-logs and journals in writing about my travels in search of endangered species, it is my hope that the reader will derive some of the satisfaction I have managed to recapture during the book's evolution. In some instances, I have interwoven into the text information about some threatened species that, although I was not privileged to witness first-hand, did occur in close proximity to the areas in which I was travelling and whose conservation is of sufficient interest and significance to record.

I shall also be well gratified if I have managed to provide the reader with a greater awareness of some of the dire problems that are at present facing the ever-increasing number of animal species that are trying to survive on earth, and for whom, in the final analysis, extinction is for ever.

· 1 ·

In Search of the Legendary Mitla

Prior to my departure from the British Isles in search of the mitla, a small press release had been issued, which had resulted in a number of interviews and a recording for the BBC's early morning programme, *Today*. From the selection of newspaper cuttings that I saw later, it was evident that none of the journalists who had interviewed me ever expected my return from what they termed as the steaming, inhospitable jungles of South America. To endorse such an appraisal, one British national paper published an article entitled: 'Zoo Man's Quest In The "Jungle Of No Return"'. It reported that a young British zoologist, employed as zoo director at Gerald Durrell's Jersey Zoo, was to make a one-man expedition into the Bolivian jungle to look for an animal that had only been seen twice. It went on to relate that Jeremy Mallinson would spend two months looking for a mitla, which was described by the explorer, Colonel Percy Fawcett, at the beginning of the century in the forests of Abuna, and which resembled a small, black, dog-like cat. In order to highlight the drama of such an expedition, catch phrases such as the 'great unknown' were played on and descriptions of the terrors of the jungle were exaggerated. It was explained that the Abuna region was near to the area Colonel Fawcett and his eldest son disappeared while they were searching for South American lost cities, and that Indian tribes who have never seen a white man hunt in the forests. The article culminated by stating that Mr Mallinson, an ex-soldier, will not take a gun and that he had said, 'I don't look at my trips as dangerous'.

Brian Fawcett, Colonel Fawcett's younger son and author of *Exploration Fawcett*, advised me during a meeting with him prior to my departure from the British Isles that I should leave all firearms behind, for they were liable to arouse suspicion; carry as little as possible; wear canvas footwear with rubber soles, for as one's feet are always likely to be wet in the forest, they would not become skinned as often as they would with leather boots; use only nylon underclothes, for they dry out quickly after immersion; avoid going into a river if I had open sores or unhealed wounds because most likely I would be devoured by piranha fish; become a habitual garlic eater to avoid being pestered by insects.

An immaculate, highly polished, chauffeur-driven ambassador's limousine collected me from the Sucre Palace Hotel at 12.20, and deftly negotiated its way in a dignified fashion through the indisciplined traffic of La Paz, to the colonial-style

residence of the British Ambassador to Bolivia, His Excellency, Mr David Crichton.

The Crichtons had arranged a luncheon in my honour and had learnt about my proposed Bolivian venture from the various press-cuttings that had been sent via the diplomatic bag from London. The contents of some of the articles had made them both curious to meet me, as well as concerned about my ultimate safety, for, as they later divulged, as I was a British citizen, if I did disappear in the forests of northern Bolivia, who would they send, and how would they know where, to look for me?

In the early part of the ambassador's diplomatic career, he had replaced Gerald Durrell's eldest brother, Lawrence, in Belgrade, so knew him reasonably well. Charles Johnson, who was in charge of the British Agricultural Mission in Bolivia, had been Director of Agriculture in Nyasaland (Malawi) prior to independence and before that had spent some twenty years in Northern Rhodesia (Zambia). It transpired that while I had served in the Rhodesia and Nyasaland Staff Corps, we had been in some of the same places and we found that we had had a number of mutual friends. Mrs Crichton told me that she had read the majority of Gerald's books and should I plan to bring back a small animal collection from the Beni province of Bolivia, she would be only too happy to accommodate them for a short time in the grounds of the embassy. I thanked her very much but warned her that the last person who had offered such facilities had done so at the time of my having accumulated a sizeable animal collection in the Okavango swamps, in 1962. As I had to transport the animals from Bechuanaland (Botswana) through

Tropical forests contain a major portion of the planet's biological diversity and some of the richest, such as many areas of pristine Amazonia rainforest, are themselves already endangered (Russell A. Mittermeier)

15

Global devastation of mature forests leaves in its wake the terminal wounds of soil erosion and a land mass denuded of productive plant life (Russell A. Mittermeier)

Southern Rhodesia (Zimbabwe), before flying the collection from Salisbury (Harare), the garden of the lady who had offered such hospitality had been taken over by various members of Africa's wildlife heritage, including a tame adult lioness, a vervet monkey, a chacma baboon, ostriches, vultures, marabou storks, African pythons and a crocodile. On learning about this, Mrs Crichton became somewhat apprehensive, but I put her mind at rest by telling her that my chief ambition was to locate a mitla and at the same time to see as much of South America's animal life in the wild as possible.

It had been H. W. Bate's *The Naturalist on the River Amazon,* which had recorded his experiences during some eleven years of travel in the mid-nineteenth century, that had originally provided me with a burning ambition to visit the Amazon basin.

Peter Fleming recorded in his classic, *Brazilian Adventure,* which provides an account of his expedition in search of Colonel Fawcett in the early 1930s, that it is always amusing and instructive to watch people's reactions when you tell them where you are going and what you plan to do once you arrive. There are the prudent who say, 'This is an extraordinarily foolish thing to do'; there are the wise who say, 'This is an extraordinarily foolish thing to do, but at least you will know better next time'; and there are the very wise who say, 'This is a foolish thing to do, but not nearly so foolish as it sounds'. My views concurred with the latter, for I had every intention of gleaning as much experience as possible from such a venture, in the understanding that my travels would provide me with a much greater awareness of the diversity and complexities of both animal and plant life, as well as the measures required for their ultimate conservation.

Colonel Fawcett recorded in his log-books that: 'In the forests were various beasts still unfamiliar to Zoologists, such as the Mitla which I have seen twice. A black dog-like cat about the size of a foxhound.' Some sixty years later, Brian Fawcett told me that his father has seen the mitla in the forests of Abuna, north of

16

Riberalta, which extend east to the Rio Mamore-Madeira. He recommended that Riberalta would be the logical place to start such an investigation and added that the possibility of their existence did not seem unreasonable, although it was strange that there was not a more general knowledge of them. However, he concluded by saying that the mitla project was an exciting one and that should I succeed in photographing such a creature, quite apart from capturing one, it would create enormous interest and would surely be a major development in zoology.

During the planning stage of the mitla venture and prior to my arrival in Bolivia, I had checked with a number of authorities to discover whether they had heard of Colonel Fawcett's legendary animal. Some of the responses provided a degree of optimism and reassurance as to the validity of my quest, whereas others were more non-commital. The anthropologist, Francis Huxley, said that it was very peculiar to find an Aztec name in South America and that, although when he undertook his studies in eastern Brazil which were recorded so excellently in his book *Affable Savages*, he did hear the Indians tell of a black jaguar which lived – partly at least – in water.

The primatologists and zoologists, W. C. Osman Hill and Ivan T. Sanderson, on my behalf, discussed in detail the possible authenticity of the mitla. Sanderson wrote:

> Is not this animal (a perhaps melanistic form) of the thing that I shot at several times but only managed to get a native legless skin of, that looked like a huge Serval, with pricked ears and tiny lynx-like tail. I believe that it was in connection with this that I heard the name 'Mixtla'.

However, both authorities were concerned about the Aztec origin of the name:

The explorer Colonel Percy Fawcett who disappeared in the jungles of Brazil in 1925 wrote in his log-book 'In the forests were various beasts still unfamiliar to Zoologists, such as a Mitla which I have seen twice – "A black dog-like cat about the size of a foxhound"'

'Mixtla' is the site of a fine Mexican temple dedicated to the god of the Underworld and such names as Caccomixtle, which were given by the Aztecs to the ring-tailed cat and meaning the cunning cat-squirrel, may have some bearing on the origin of the mixtla. Osman Hill wished me every success with my venture, and Ivan Sanderson recommended that I should get in touch with Bernard Heuvelman on the mitla question.

Bernard Heuvelman had just published his classic *On the Track of Unknown Animals*, to which Gerald Durrell had written the foreword for the English edition. He said that he had not included the mitla or mixtla in his book for he thought in reality it might be an animal unknown to Colonel Fawcett but not to zoology. He cited the tayra, or a melanistic form of one of the several South American tiger cats, or even the peculiar jaguarundi which is sometimes completely black. The only information that he had on a tall, unknown cat-like animal in western Amazonia had been described as 'half pig, half jaguar'. However, he concluded by saying that it was quite possible that the mitla was still an undescribed animal and that he could only wish me good luck and a good hunt.

The Lloyd Aereo Boliviano plane lifted itself sluggishly, like an over-indulged Condor, from the highest international airport in the world, which is situated approximately 305m (1,000ft) above La Paz, and is some 4,115m (13,500ft) above sea level on the high plateau (Altiplano) of the Andean range. In spite of the altitude, the aircraft was over-shadowed by the majestic snow-capped 6,400m (21,000ft) summit of Mount Illimani, which was spectacularly profiled against the intense blue sky. Just to the north-west could be seen the blue-emerald water of Lake Titicaca, known as the 'Sacred Lake', which represents the world's highest navigable lake and which plays host to such unique creatures as the flightless Titicaca grebe and the baggy-looking Lake Titicaca frog.

Leaving the snow-capped mountains to the west, the plane flew over the more arid mountainous terrain of the Andean foothills and descended to Cochabamba, Bolivia's second largest city; as it represents the centre of the country's richest agricultural region and supplies Bolivia with the majority of its fruit and potatoes, it is known as the 'Barn of Bolivia'.

It was within a small valley in the south-eastern district of Cochabamba on the eastern slopes of the Andes that the red-fronted macaw was first described. Robert Ridgely, an American ornithologist, was the first ever to see the species in the wild, considering it to have the smallest range of any macaw. When Rolando Romero of Santa Cruz had seen a captive specimen for the first time, he had thought it might have been a hybrid between the military macaw and the blue and white macaw, its body being mainly pale green and its forehead, crown, ear-coverts, shoulders, under-coverts and thighs orange-red; the tail is red and blue and the bill is black.

Although the red-fronted macaw was at this time considered to be the rarest of the macaws, a study by Dirk Lanning estimated a wild population of between three and five thousand. As little of the macaw's preferred habitat is suitable for agriculture and their nesting sites are not vulnerable because of their utilisation of sandstone cliffs which are inaccessible to collectors, it had been concluded that only if commercial trappers and exporters moved into this restricted area would the wild population become threatened. Regrettably, since the time of my visit to the Cochabamba region, one exporter has estimated that three hundred red-

The red-fronted macaw
was first described within
a small valley on the
eastern slopes on the
Andes in Bolivia. Due to
its preferred habitat
being not suitable for
agriculture, only the
presence of trappers has
resulted in the
elimination of this
threatened species' adult
breeding population each
year (Phillip Coffey)

fronted macaws left Bolivia in one year, and that trappers operating in the northern half of the macaw's range, because of the restricted area concerned, are eliminating part of the adult breeding population each year.

While I was in this area of the Andes, I enquired whether there had been any recent sightings of South America's only representative of the bear family, the spectacled bear. We had already represented this species in the Jersey collection and were anxious to develop a captive breeding programme as the wild population was becoming increasingly endangered. Sparsely distributed in the mountainous areas of western Venezuela, in Colombia, Ecuador, Peru and northern Bolivia, this attractive animal is moderately tolerant of variations in the altitude, climate and vegetation of its habitat. Although it is typically tree-living in the forest, it is equally adaptable to relatively arid environments.

The diet of the spectacled bear consists mainly of vegetables and fruit and its climbing ability is especially developed for picking its food. The principal characteristic that differentiates the spectacled bear from other black bears is the whitish or yellowish mask that adorns the muzzle; the mask sometimes comes in the form of distinct spectacles around the eyes and cheeks whereas some have white markings under the eyes and a creamy coloured muzzle.

Wherever the spectacled bear's habitat has been taken over for any type of cultivation or development, it is evident that its numbers have been greatly depleted and in some cases disappeared completely. Although supposedly illegal, it was possible to acquire a much-prized skin within a month once a deposit had been paid. It seemed all too easy to secure such a trophy, thus causing the death of this endearing creature.

After leaving Cochabamba the twin-prop Aero Boliviano plane made a number of stops on earthen landing strips, putting down at Trinidad, Santa Ana, Guayaramerin and finally at Riberalta. In some of the situations, it was difficult to discern whether the plane was skimming dangerously over the jungle canopy and about to do a forced landing or not, for the pilot seemed to find landing strips in the most unlikely places.

The jungle canopy was one endless flat carpet, interwoven with every shade of green imaginable. The snaking, muddy rivers flowed lethargically away from the Andes to the north-east, some of which took the most ridiculous of courses. As we flew at low level over some of the remotest tributaries of the Amazon network, small weed-clogged riverines could be detected disappearing into dark tunnels of the embracing jungle. Occasionally, the vivid purple-blue colouring of a group of jacaranda trees could be seen, as if they were embroidered on the green carpet of the canopy, which provided a welcome contrast to the cloaked forested regions beneath.

Prior to my arrival in Bolivia, I had corresponded with Perry Priest, the Bolivian Director of the Instituto Linguistico de Verano (ILV) concerning my quest for the mitla, and told him that I wanted to travel to the Abuna forest region. He replied that they would be willing to fly me, for a nominal fee, to a jungle landing-strip called Nacebe, which was situated between the Rio Beni and Rio Abuna, and that there was a trail from the landing-strip which would take me into the area where I could commence my investigations. He told me to make wireless contact with him once I had arrived in Riberalta, so, once I had landed there and found my hotel, I went in search of the wireless communications office.

A multitude of lugubrious fish species thrive within the muddy-complexioned waters of the Amazon basin providing valuable protein food for local inhabitants

Riberalta consisted of a series of mud and clay plastered single-storey buildings that were arranged in blocks, their roofs covered by rusty corrugated iron sheetings. In the centre of the township, the foundations of the buildings jutted out in order to provide a solid raised pavement, about 30–60cm (1–2ft) above the red-brown earthen tracks, Some of the buildings had verandah roofing extended over the pavement to provide both shade from the intensity of the sun and shelter from the tropical downfalls that were just starting to manifest themselves.

The township is only approximately 152m (500ft) above sea level and had been built on the site of an old entrenched Indian village, at the confluence of the Beni and Madre de Dias rivers. From all appearances, it could not have altered much from the time Colonel Fawcett visited it on a number of occasions at the turn of the century, at the height of the boom in the rubber trade. At that time, Fawcett described how two of the big rubber firms in Riberalta kept forces of armed men for hunting the forest Indians, in order to capture and organise them as slave labour to work the wild rubber; wholesale butchery was commonplace, as well as the meting out of lashings for anyone who attempted to disobey an order or to escape from their enslavement.

The great distance of the rubber-producing regions from any effective state control encouraged the more unscrupulous and degenerate members of society and as drink and gambling were a way of life, most people found it difficult to keep out of debt and to be untouched by the vices of their community. Colonel Fawcett concluded:

Surrounded by brutality and bestial passions, living in unbelievable squalor, isolated by vast distances, lack of communication and impossible jungle, it is not surprising that people sought escape in the only way they know – by means of the bottle.

The telegraph office was situated in the midst of a trading store and I was relieved to find that the proprietor, Señor Carlos, could speak excellent English. I showed him a copy of my communication with Perry Priest and he told me to return at 8.15 the following morning when his daily wireless contact with ILV took place. In the meantime, he would be pleased to show me his collection of animal skins that he had received from trappers and other traders.

I told him about my search for the mitla and showed him an identikit picture of the legendary animal that had been illustrated and painted onto a ceramic tile. He informed me that he occasionally had skins brought to him of a black canine-feline animal. These cats, which were found in the forests were called *gato eyra* and were considered to be black mutations of the jaguarundi – it was an interesting lead. He had not always been able to identify other skins that were brought to him. Although he had never heard the name 'mitla' or 'mixtla' associated with them, he thought that the name could be Peruvian as it certainly was not of Bolivian origin.

I photographed a good cross-section of Señor Carlos' collection of skins, which included those of jaguar, ocelot, various small spotted cats, river otter and caiman. In one corner of the shop lay a large pile of vicuna skins that were in transit to another dealer, the skins having only just recently been transported from La Paz. Having previously learnt that the vicuna together with the chinchilla were the only two animals listed by the Bolivian authorities as being on a restricted list, I tried to discover as much information as possible on the amount of trade in vicuna that was obviously taking place.

According to the trader, there was no restriction on the export of vicuna wool or wool waste, and that the current price of the wool, or at least its export value, was US $2.2 per kilo (2.2lb) on which, since 1961, the government had levied a 15 per cent export tax. Señor Carlos had heard a rumour that the Ministero de Hacienda was going to restrict the total annual export figure and also the number of people allowed to shoot vicuna. He informed me that many skins were smuggled over the border from Peru and were welcomed by the Bolivian authorities because of the tax that was levied on their re-exportation. Señor Carlos had been told that much of the vicuna fleece was collected by driving the herds through cactus and then collecting the entangled wool. In theory, the idea was laudable, but it was easy to sense that Señor Carlos was as disbelieving as myself regarding the authenticity of the story, particularly as I had heard reports that machine-guns were used to hunt vicuna on the altiplano. At that time, the survival of the Bolivian economy, like that of many other countries in the developing world, relied heavily on trade with the outside world, and interest in wild animals was stimulated only if there was an end product by way of skin or edible meat. Fortunately, through education, the work of international conservation agencies and international legislation governing the trade of endangered species which arose from the Washington Convention (known as CITES), the trafficking of wild animal products has almost come to a standstill. In the mid-1980s, the Bolivian government prohibited the hunting, capture, harassment, transport, sale, transfer

and export of live wild animals and their parts, which highlights what can be achieved once there is a general awareness regarding the value and importance of conservation measures.

Twenty-one years after *Oryx* the journal of the Fauna and Flora Preservation Society published my article describing the problems facing the vicuna species in Bolivia, it is significant that successful experiences in vicuna capture and shearing have been carried out recently with the help of New Zealand technicians, which has resulted in some 3,500kg (7,700lb) of vicuna wool being held in stock in Peru. More than 2,000 vicuna have been translocated from the Pampa Galeras Reserve over distances of 1,000km (600 miles) with a casualty rate of only ½ per cent.

Now that safe techniques for the capture, translocation and shearing of wild animals are available, it is hoped that the local people may begin to benefit from the presence of vicuna on their lands. Dr Felipe Benavides, Chairman of the Vicuna Commission in Peru, is actively working with the International Union for Conservation and Natural Resources (IUCN) and CITES, with the help of international lawyers with the Peruvian Ambassador in Switzerland, to create a

The spectacled bear is the only representative of the bear in South America. Wherever its habitat has been taken over for cultivation and development this endangered species has either disappeared completely or its numbers greatly reduced

situation whereby vicuna cloth, sheared from live vicuna and woven in Peru, will be legally on sale again. After many years of striving to secure remnant wild populations of threatened species, international conservationists have made advances so that the animals can be farmed as a renewable resource for the benefit of the local people.

Just before sunset I left Señor Carlos' trading store and made my way back along the dusty road-cum-track to the Riberalta Hotel. It was hot and muggy, and my heart went out to the spanned-oxen as they hauled their solid wooden-wheeled carts that creaked on their unlubricated, over-laden axles, while their expressionless, dispassionate drivers constantly flicked the hinds of the oxen with the aid of crude-looking knotted rawhide whips. A few of the wealthier residents trotted past on mule-back, their Western-style saddles and canyon-like stirrups resembling a scene from an early Hollywood Western more than a current-day happening.

Next morning, I rose just after first light, anxious to escape from the stale air and mugginess of my surroundings. I left the hotel and, to the rear of it, followed a red mud-path down to the Rio Beni. After passing a few thatch-plumed mud-huts of the river Indians and a variety of mongrel dogs, which approached me to sniff, bark and then scratch, I reached a good vantage point on the south bank of the Beni which provided my first view from the ground of one of the thousand or so tributaries of the largest river in the world. This was part of the luxuriant, forest-covered Amazon wilderness which extends some 6.5 million sq km (2½ million sq miles) across two-fifths of South America, north and south of the equator, the majority of the region representing a flat river basin less than 198m (650ft) above sea level.

An extravagantly plumed scarlet macaw flew noisily from one part of the riverine undergrowth to some fruit trees near some Indian dwellings, while a number of pencil-shaped wooden dug-outs were being skilfully navigated by their

The vicuna fleece represents the most luxuriant and valuable of all wool products. Through a properly regulated management system it is hoped that local people may soon begin to benefit from the presence of vicuna on their lands (Fauna & Flora Preservation Society)

paddlers through the swollen waters, before they went out of sight around a bend in the river upstream, doubtless to undertake their daily quest for fish.

It was soon time to keep my appointment at the trading store and to learn from the radio link with ILV how soon the institute could fly me north to Nacebe. Exactly at 8am, Señor Carlos made radio contact with one of the pilots at the institute, who told him that Perry Priest was at present away in Cochabamba and that he did not know anything about Mr Mallinson's search for a legendary animal called a mitla. However, as he was about to fly down to Riberalta, he suggested that I should meet him on the landing-strip at 10 o'clock.

On my way to the air-strip, I came across a small but neatly maintained Roman Catholic church and thought that this would be as good a time as any to pay my more formal respects to the Almighty, and seek both guidance and good fortune. The exterior of the church was pastel-blue in colour, whereas the interior was well ventilated and appeared to be as white as a freshly laundered cassock. Wood-carved stations-of-the-cross and garlanded pictures of a selection of saints adorned the walls, while a massive wooden crucifix left no worshipper in doubt as to which house of religious denomination they had just entered. As so often is the case, such trappings of the original European settlers and empires are usually the only aspect of such settlements that are still able to maintain themselves, because of various financial injections from the outside world.

Very much on schedule, the one-engined Piper-Aztec landed on the grass verge of the muddy landing-strip and taxied over the ground's bumpy undulations. A young American pilot clambered out of the cockpit and introduced himself by stating that his name was Chuck. After I had shown him my correspondence with his director and had explained my eagerness to commence my search for the mitla in the Abuna regions, he informed me that the institute's second plane was being serviced and that as the servicing of his plane was already overdue, he did not believe that I could be flown to Nacebe for at least a further two to two-and-a-half weeks.

I returned to Señor Carlos' trading store in order to benefit from his advice as he had shown an increasing amount of interest in my investigations of the mitla and had offered help if it was required. He spread out on the floor of his verandah a large, but undetailed, map of the north-eastern border of Bolivia with Brazil, and, after much discussion, advocated that I should take the Lloyd Aero Boliviano flight that afternoon to Guayaramerin, which is on the west bank of the Rio Mamore. From there, I could cross the river to Guajara-Mirim on the Brazilian side, and then it would be comparatively easy to make my way to Villa Murtinho, which is situated adjacent to the confluence of the Rio Beni with the Mamore. Once the two waters merge, the river takes on the name of Rio Madeira which, together with the Rio Negro, represent the two major tributaries of the Amazon. Each of these vast waterways disgorge at their mouth as much water as Africa's Zaire river which, measured by volume, after the Amazon, is regarded as the world's second largest river; such is the unrivalled immensity of the Amazonas, which are reputed to pour into the Atlantic one-fifth of all the river water on earth.

Señor Carlos explained that, on arrival at Villa Murtinho, I should be able to hire some type of craft with its owner and to work my way upstream, exploring some of the lesser tributaries that flowed into the Beni from the north, for I had already established during my previous discussions with Brian Fawcett that it was

The thatch-plumed mud-
huts of the river dwellers
are arranged in clusters
along the shore lines,
each family being lords of
their respective domains

probably in this region, between the Beni and the Rio Abuna to the north, that his
father had encountered the mitla. Señor Carlos recommended that, if I did not
meet with any type of success in those regions, I could return to Villa Murtinho
and travel north to Abunan, which was opposite to the Rio Abuna's confluence
with the Madeira, and carry out similar investigatory work in that area. Like a
jigsaw puzzle, my plans were now falling into place and, with Señor Carlos'
guidance and help, I was able to acquire a ticket for the twice-weekly plane to
Guajara-Mirim.

Guajara-Mirim was a back-door into Brazil and it was soon evident that
travellers such as myself were seldom to be encountered, so this was to be a feast
day. It was the contents of my outward-bound rucksack that caused the most
interest, for the official examined every article with the same enthusiasm and
fastidiousness as if he had just been presented with the contents of a treasure-
chest. The four packages of one-man, two-day emergency rations, each pack
consisting of 5,167 calories, in waterproof wrappings; water-sterilisation tablets;
army torch and batteries, attached to a khaki web-belt; concentrated fuel cubes;
garlic cloves and insect-repellent liquid; general-purpose soap, which lathered in
any type of water; a pouch containing my MK IV prismatic compass; army issue
foot and body powder; the all-weather sleeping-bag with its 'fitex' waterproof

26

Work of the Jersey Wildlife Preservation Trust

Les Augrès Manor is the home of the Jersey Wildlife Preservation Trust, which was founded by Gerald Durrell in 1963 as a unique centre for the breeding of rare and endangered species of animals in captivity. Now the Trust headquarters is the centre of a worldwide organisation, with two supporting associations, Wildlife Preservation Trust International in America, and Wildlife Preservation Trust Canada, that are united in the common goals of preserving endangered wildlife through carefully controlled breeding programmes, promoting field-work and research into these species' requirements, developing partnerships with govern-ments to protect and conserve the animals in the wild, and to communicate the Trust's work through public and professional education programmes to a wider audience around the world.

By promoting national, regional and international co-operation and co-ordination, supporting 'on site' captive breeding programmes, aiding the training of selected personnel, and instigating field research and re-introduction projects, the Wildlife Preservation Trusts have helped to further the establishment of survival reservoirs for endangered species and to promote the conservation role of a modern zoo.

The Jersey Trust has instigated species survival plans for such endangered animals as the golden-headed lion tamarin, Rodrigues fruit bat, Jamaican hutia, white eared pheasant, Meller's duck, St Lucia parrot, Mauritius pink pigeon, Waldrapp ibis, keel-scaled boa, Round Island skink and gecko, radiated tortoise and Majorcan midwife toad; as well as having a great many other breeding populations of threatened and endangered species represented in its collection.

With over 20,000 members in some 72 different countries, the Wildlife Preservation Trust would welcome further support for its many activities in aid of species survival.   (Photo: Philip Coffey)

Packages of one-man, two-day emergency rations, water sterilisation tablets, snake-bite serum, a Mk IV prismatic compass, were all part of the paraphernalia that in an emergency one could not do without

sleeve and mosquito-net hood; a camera, in its waterproof rubber bag and 'sileka-gel' innards, and binoculars – all represented essentials that I considered I could not be without.

The *pièce de résistance* for the official were the contents of one of the waterproof zip-pockets. Among such items was a small carving of an African's head, which had been my lucky charm ever since I was given it before I went to the Belgian Congo some eight years previously, and an assortment of family photographs, which also included one of my favourite lowland gorilla at the Jersey Trust, N'Pongo, and one of the mitla identikit.

Somewhat mesmerised by this assortment of artifacts and illustrations, the official decided to terminate any further examination of my personal gear, and I was motioned to repack my belongings, my passport was stamped, and I was allowed to go on my way into Brazil, free to travel wherever I wanted in this lush heart of South America.

·2·

The Pacahuaras Hold on to their Secrets

ALTHOUGH the River Beni was, perhaps, at its lowest level of the year, in midstream the current had been quite persuasive, so the cigar-shaped boat, with its heavy load of provisions and two passengers, had to hug the river's southern shore in order to make any real progress upstream. As we passed a small gathering of dwellings nestled into the elbow of the Beni with the mainstream of the Mamore-Madeira rivers, the Brazilian boatman had pointed at the place acclaiming, 'Villa Bella', but there was little to commend it from the river, so we avoided stopping there.

Partially submerged relics of boats appeared to stud the foreground, while houses built on stilts afforded shade for numerous children, small packs of mongrel dogs and countless poultry, which, among a quantity of garbage, seemed to pepper the shoreline like termites. Colonel Fawcett had described Villa Bella in his logs as 'Reeking in undisguised filth, its inhabitants drink-sodden and degenerate'. It appeared to have changed very little during the past sixty years and I was relieved once the mantle of the forest had started to take over from the obvious poverty and degradation of this transient stage, between the threshold of civilisation and that of the natural world.

Before leaving the small river settlement of Villa Murtinho, I engaged the services of a bright-eyed Brazilian youth and agreed to pay his father 10,000 cruzeiros per day. I had no idea as to how much I was being overcharged, but as any alternative was unlikely, there was little else for me to do but accept the terms. I provided Claudio with some additional funds in order to purchase and load into the boat as many provisions, and fuel for the Japanese outboard motor, as it could carry, and I arranged with him to start the journey just after first light the following morning.

Before my departure, I had become increasingly concerned at how little I knew about the areas into which I was about to travel. Would some of the Indian tribes have collections of skins that I could look at, and if so, would any of these yield some type of evidence as to the mitla's authenticity? There was even the possibility that the word mitla belonged to one of the remote tribes inhabiting the forest regions between the Beni and the Abuna.

At almost half-hourly intervals for approximately five minutes, Claudio rested his treasured outboard motor, which apparently was essential if his boat was to continue to make such good progress upstream. In some places in these lower

regions, the Beni was about 400m (¼ mile) wide and its muddy waters effectively shielded the diversity of its exotic world of freshwater fish beneath. The most numerous representative of the animal kingdom was an amazing galaxy of butterflies. As we hugged the bank, they could be seen affixed to the overhanging branches of the trees like colourful Christmas decorations; then, on becoming disturbed by the noisy outboard, they would let down their translucent wings and fly effortlessly to another invisible attraction. Some of the smaller ones ranged from a lemon-barley to a mustard colouring, and when one of the much larger and more impressive bluish-purple species flew into their midst, they would scatter like small birds in the presence of a sparrow-hawk.

During our first day on the river, we travelled upstream for a period of up to six hours. I had spent the majority of my time sitting sideways on the middle seat of the boat, with both my binoculars and camera at the ready. Although Claudio had had a siesta during a long midday stop, I decided that it would be prudent to call an early stop for this first day, so that I could organise a daily routine to establish camp and arrange the main meal of the twenty-four hours.

Fortunately, Claudio immediately adopted the role of cook and succeeded in boiling up some rice mixed with the ubiquitous black beans which, if nothing else, suffocated any pangs of hunger. Whereas I had my sleeping-bag, mosquito net and waterproof cover to arrange either on the floorboards of a deserted hut or on some high ground, Claudio preferred to make his sleeping place on the downstream side of the boat which, wherever possible, we dragged onto a nearby sand-bank. As it seemed to have a habit of raining at night, I kept my kit-bag and other belongings shrouded in polythene and soon wondered how any traveller could have previously been without it. When darkness fell like a theatre curtain on a stage, I had taken refuge under my mosquito net and spent the initial few hours of my first night sleeping rough in an Amazonian forest completely mesmerised by the orchestrations that issued from the animal kingdom's nocturnal players.

The phosphorescent glimmering forms of the agile firefly picked their way

through the walls of vegetation, seemingly bringing messages of enlightenment from one area of the forest to another. Feline-like noises pierced the pinging and belching overtures of the river's amphibian life, but I could not connect the specific calls to a jaguar, ocelot or to the smaller tiger cats that were known to inhabit such regions. It appeared that the forests were bursting with life, while its inmates preferred to hunt and play under the cool covering of darkness, resting up during the heat of the day.

It was the dawn chorus of a troupe of howler monkeys that quickly brought me to my senses at first light, but although their deep roaring vocalisation, promoting their territorial defiance to other groups in the vicinity, appeared to be within a few feet of me, I was unable to catch a glimpse of them in their domain of the middle and upper storeys of the surrounding forest.

Before long, we were back on the Beni and soon passed a small village, marked on the map as Provenir, its stilted-houses and surrounding debris of the outside world badly scarring the back-drop of the green walls of vegetation. Apart from the half-hourly short stops when the boat was nosed into the bank and I usually stepped ashore to upset unintentionally a small cloud of butterflies, we had motored for almost five hours before stopping at midday. Although the outboard motor had now consumed over half of its fuel reserves, we had made good progress and had come across an attractive grouping of thatched, stilted-dwellings, nestled into a small clearing on the north bank. As we landed, a small family group of Bolivian-Indian stock looked at us with obvious apprehension, before Claudio spoke to them in a tongue that was certainly neither Spanish nor Portuguese, and whatever he related to them caused their consternation to dissolve into smiles. As I had heard Claudio make mention of the mitla, I produced the identikit tile but, although they all viewed it with the utmost interest, they showed not the slightest sign of having recognised something that they had either heard of, or were acquainted with, before.

During my few weeks of river travel, the reaction whenever I produced the identikit tile was almost always the same: an initial curiosity, an attempt to touch it and then a lot of broad smiles. However, these river-dwellers were among the most hospitable people that I had ever encountered. Most were only able to eke out an existence for themselves, yet, provided they sensed that the stranger in their midst was not there to exploit them, they would share their food and their dwelling without expecting anything in return. It was a humbling experience and totally devoid of the materialism of the Western world.

Most of these river-dwellers stuck to the disastrous cycle of 'burn, sow, move and burn', but they normally kept to the banks of the rivers and penetrated little into the surrounding forests. In some cases, the river-dwellers still tapped the latex from the wild rubber trees, the maze of waterways acting as their highways and lanes through the densely vegetated regions. It was between Puerto Lopez and Buen Retiro that we attempted to penetrate deeper into the forest to the north of the Beni. Although I had the most up-to-date map of this area, it seemed to be devoid of any waterways other than the main arteries of the Amazon network.

With hindsight, it had been fortunate that I had not had any real idea of the type of confrontations I would encounter in such remote regions of northern Bolivia for, if I had fully recognised the basic implications of such travels, I would probably not have launched myself, so unrehearsed, into some of the areas that I attempted to negotiate. The further we travelled from the Beni, the more nervous Claudio became. However, I soon learnt that the best way to counteract such apprehension was to produce my Mark IV prismatic compass, take a bearing and then make an entry in my log.

During the daytime, I wore as little as possible. This was not just because of the frequent intense heat and humidity, but as we ventured further into the forest's interior, the more often did we have to jump overboard in order to negotiate the boat around sand- and mud-banks, as well as past fallen trees. As the green walls of vegetation started to close in around us, in some places the branches reached across the waterway in their quest for more light, creating a canopy which in turn cast clouds of welcoming shade beneath.

Owing to the increased shallowness of the tributary which, on a number of occasions, had caused the outboard's propeller to become entangled and to jar against various obstacles, much to Claudio's relief the motor was retired and the boat's progress had to rely on our paddling. Although this proved to be much more demanding, such additional effort was well compensated by the stillness and tranquillity of the surroundings, as well as providing me with the opportunity to absorb fully the beauty and benefit from the solace of the environment. Although the butterfly kingdom appeared to have usurped all other groups of animals, its members were sometimes as apparent as spring blossoms falling from an orchard in a lively wind; their flutterings were sometimes interrupted by crested Amazon kingfishers as they skimmed over the water through their midst, displaying vivid flashes of blue before diving with unswerving accuracy into the murky water, where, more often than not, they secured a sizeable prey.

On one occasion, I was fortunate enough to catch a brief glimpse of the dark brown form of a Brazilian tapir, as it was gathering itself out of the river and up a

The combination of water and undisturbed habitats are essential to the tapir's existence

steep bank until it disapperared into the embrace of the forest. The tapir family is represented by a single living genus comprising four species, three of which exist in parts of South and Central America, and one, the Malayan tapir, in south-east Asia. Tapirs are the only living representatives in the New World of the order of mammals Perissodactyla (odd-toed ungulates) which includes horses, asses, zebras and rhinoceroses. The existence of a tapir in the higher parts of the northern Andes was known since the early years of the Spanish occupation, but was assumed to be the same animal as the lowland form. The mountain tapir was first described as a distinct species in 1829 by Roulin, and this smallest of the four species is also known as the woolly, hairy, Andean, or Roulin's, tapir. The Central American, or Baird's, tapir is a more stoutly built animal about the size of a donkey, and its habitat comprises damp tropical forests ranging from marshy lowland to montane forest up to a high altitude.

The combination of water and undisturbed habitats are essential to the tapir's existence as it is completely at home in water and spends much time wallowing. If pursued, it takes refuge in a river, lake or swamp for it is an excellent swimmer and can remain submerged for a considerable period of time. As tapirs are shy and cannot tolerate disturbance by man or his domestic animals, both the mountain and Baird's tapirs are now listed in the IUCN red list of threatened animals. Although the Brazilian tapir has a wide distribution in South America, it is constantly hunted and regarded as a delicacy by the local people. In some cases, young tapirs are caught and reared until they are old enough to provide food for the family.

As I ticked off the days in my log book, our progress became increasingly hindered by the shallowness of the water and the riverines became increasingly interrupted by fallen trees and sand-banks. Once the wet season had really got under way, no doubt the sand-banks would be covered and the logs brushed aside by the reinvigorated currents. If our way became too blocked, we would go downstream again before trying another, lesser tributary. In spite of the fact that none of these waterways were marked on my map, I started to develop a curious kind of indifference, becoming almost flippant as to the chances of becoming lost, having an accident, or to the possibility of Claudio disappearing downstream one night with his boat. Perhaps it was a combination of not having recently made contact with any river-dwellers in these regions, the lack of any real progress northwards to put me within striking distance of the south bank of the Rio Abuna, the fact that our food rations had gone down by approximately two-thirds, that made me decide that it was time to follow the currents downstream, return to Villa Murtinho and then travel north to the Rio Abuna.

It took some two-and-a-half days to get back to the Beni, although I did take the opportunity to make some further investigations at various different groups of stilted-houses, in order to check with the local inhabitants whether they possessed any skins that resembled a mitla. I also showed a selected number of the river-dwellers the identikit tile, in the hope that somebody would recognise such an animal; but alas, no one showed the slightest glimmer of ever having seen such a species. On the evening prior to reaching the Beni, I accepted an offer to stay the night with a large family in one of the stilted-houses. Just after sunset, we shared some of our rations and when I produced a tin of condensed milk, it was received with the same degree of appreciation as if I had just produced a bottle of select

malt whisky. Although Claudio retired to his usual position by the boat, I remained with the family group of some eleven individuals, together with their pet squirrel monkey. I slept on the stilted-platform as a part of the community and did not experience any inhibitions at the close proximity of some of my fellow slumberers.

Our arrival at the riverine's confluence with the Beni acted as a signal for Claudio to use his outboard motor again, restart the engine and use up the remainder of our limited fuel supplies. We arrived back at Villa Murtinho almost exactly three weeks after we had set out and although no further light had been shone on the mitla legend, a great deal had been learnt about the deep-rooted mystiques that surround these somewhat sombre forest enclaves.

While reclaiming my cachet of belongings from the police station, I met up with Professor Gaston Bejarano and a New Zealander by the name of Ian D. Hutchinson. The latter was leading a small Bolivian expedition, recording for FAO the many different types of trees that were to be found in the forests of this particular region of north-eastern Bolivia. Although the party had travelled extensively within the Beni and Abuna area, they had neither seen nor heard reference to an animal resembling the mitla. Professor Bejarano strongly supported the suggestion that the mitla could be a melanistic form of the jaguarundi, as in these denser regions of the forest, where little light manages to filter through to the ground, black forms of various smaller carnivores are frequently encountered.

There are numerous different species of Amazon parrots that are largely green, stockily built and blunt-tailed which blend easily within their forest homeland

I explained my plans to travel north to the Abuna and to try to make contact with members of the Pacahuara tribe, whom I had been told would be almost certain to know about the mitla's authenticity. The professor informed me that the Pacahuara were now considered to be less sociable than they had been a hundred years ago, when the tribesmen were hunted like animals and, when caught, brought back as slaves to tap the wild rubber trees for their ruthless overseers. For these reasons, they had retreated into the heart of the forests, keeping away from the main waterways and maintaining a low profile.

The following morning I accepted the invitation to travel north to Abuna with Gaston Bejarano and Ian Hutchinson. As the Brazilian jeep picked its way along the dusty track, the heat of the day seemed to be far more oppressive than it had been when we had travelled on the numerous waterways, for there always appeared to be a slight breeze that was funnelled between the thick walls of vegetation on either bank. By the time we reached the hotel in Abuna, which turned out to be a slightly larger version of the one in Villa Murtinho, with the same trappings of dirt and vermin, we decided to strip and bathe in the Rio Madeira, as opposed to chancing any bathing facility that the hotel had to offer, even though we were covered with the dust and grime of the journey.

Prior to Ian Hutchinson's and Gaston Bajarano's departure to Porto Velho the following morning, they took me to the small police station and introduced me to the inspector in charge. He agreed to help me acquire a boat and its owner, but stated that it would not be possible to hire an outboard motor, for such engines were extremely scarce in this particular region.

Ilmar was a much sturdier man than Claudio, but appeared to have the ability to paddle for a long period of time without having to keep stopping for a rest. Fortunately, Ilmar could easily manoeuvre his boat without having to rely on my assistance, but whenever I was not feasting my eyes on the surroundings, I aided the boat's progress with a spoon-like paddle from my position near to the bows. Rice, black beans, water melons, hands of bananas, a water container and our respective personal belongings filled the rest of the craft, and, because of such a load, I reflected how fortunate we were to be going upstream on the Abuna when its current was at its lowest seasonal level.

The Abuna proved to be much narrower than the Beni and after the small settlement of Manoa on the south bank, it took on a zig-zagging course, flowing from the north and then from the south. Colonel Fawcett had mapped the source of the Abuna at the beginning of the century, but before doing so, had been told to look after himself on the river because: 'The fever there will kill you and if you escape that, there are the dreaded Pacahuara Indians'. Although everything that I had heard about the Abuna had endowed it with an evil reputation, I consoled myself by thinking of Peter Flemming's search for Fawcett, when he had written, 'Exploring in Matto Grosso is a soft option compared with caravanning in the Cotswolds', and I appreciated that so much in life was undoubtedly relative to how much one allows one's mind to fantasise. So I preoccupied myself with the region's natural history and only now and again weighed up the pros and cons of the mitla's authenticity.

Our initial progress on the Abuna was painfully slow in comparison to a similar period of time on the Beni. Whenever we reached any type of small riverine or stream entering the Abuna from the south, I would take the opportunity to stop at any of the stilted-dwellings and, through Ilmar, ask to examine any animal skins that they had, and only prior to our departure would I take the opportunity to show them the identikit tile of the mitla. I always enjoyed such interactions but became increasingly aware that I was wasting my time in showing the tile, and that perhaps my only chance of gleaning any evidence about Fawcett's legendary animal would be through the examination of the river trader's collection of skins.

Although pet monkeys and parrots were often to be seen in the houses of the river-dwellers, on one occasion I saw a young marmoset belonging to a species that I failed to identify. It had a length of thin twine around its waist and when I approached it to take photographs, its shrill and rapid vocalisation reminded me of a pair of saddle-back tamarins, with which we formed a small family group at the Jersey Zoo. However, whereas the infant and juvenile markings of the saddle-back tamarin young at Jersey had been predominantly black, this three-to-four-month-old juvenile had a blaze of white across its forehead, half-moons of white covering each cheek pouch framing the nostrils and remarkably alert black eyes. The rest of the body, including the crown of its head, the nape of its neck, its mantle and tail, was black. It was only after my return to Jersey and through sending a photograph of the specimen to a number of primate specialists, that it was eventually identified by Philip Herschkovitz of the Field Museum of Natural History, Chicago, who recognised it as a juvenile specimen of the Weddell's saddle-back tamarin *Saguinus fuscicollis weddelli.*

In places, we came across small islands of luxuriant vegetation. Lianas, twisted like cables among the roughened tree trunks, were often studded by a great diversity of epiphytes – air plants that flourish in such a humid atmosphere. The buttress bases of the trees had evolved to cope with the seasonal floodings, while their lofty tops continued their ceaseless search for light, space and moisture. At times, the heavens opened and it was almost impossible to see more than a few yards ahead; then, when the downpour was over and sunlight filtered through the forest canopy among the damp green foliage and hanging creepers, it was like being within nature's luxuriant hot-house. As the vast walls of forest sponged up the moisture with their insatiable thirst, the temperature rose and one's body and clothes were soon dried.

After some three days of travelling, we arrived at the river settlement of José Gormez. News of our presence in this region had preceded us and we were greeted by what appeared to be a small reception committee. There was the usual amount of quarrelsome, skeletal mongrel dogs, a good representation of poultry scratching in the ground and a sizeable population of children under the age of nine. No one had heard the name mitla, none of the skins I examined belonged to any unknown species, and when I produced the identikit tile, I received the now customary amount of amusement. With regard to the Pacahuara Indians, the residents of José Gormez obviously had a healthy respect for them and did not wish to become involved, even by talking about them.

We stayed the night at José Gormez and, after taking our leave the following morning, kept well into the south bank and commenced our progress against the current upstream. The Abuna was now less twisting in its course and in places its banks consisted of somewhat forbidding forest walls, with its trees towering some 20–30m (22–33yd) to the dense canopy; this back-drop to the muddy-complexioned river was only occasionally interrupted by lone jacarandas that punctuated the sea of green vegetation. Much of the journey was in silence and I had the pleasure of witnessing such aspects of natural history as the ubiquitous butterflies, discordant parties of parrots and many other species of Amazon bird and animal noises in the wilderness of the forest.

After some eight days of travelling, while we were looking for a suitable place to land, much to my surprise I picked out through my binoculars a flag hanging limply from a sapling that improvised as a flag-post. Near the flag-post, on the river bank, a small group of men dressed in denim-type uniform were gathered together. Once we came closer to the clearing, a notice informed us that the camp was a 'Districto Militer Boliviano', which consisted of some twenty soldiers and two officers.

This small military base on Bolivia's northern border was one of the most isolated of its kind. Across the Abuna, there were hundreds of square miles of dense forests belonging to Brazil. On each side of the clearing in which the camp was sited, which included a rough landing-strip, stretched another, almost impenetrable, barrier of foliage on the Bolivian side of the international boundary between these two, little-penetrated backwaters of the Amazon network. The only contact with the outside world was by way of a small radio transmitter and receiver, which the wireless operator tuned in to at 7.15am each day, and spoke to a check-point to the south.

Our arrival seemed to take the camp by surprise, for seldom had any European travelled into this remote area. I greeted the captain with the only Spanish I could remember, *Fala Inglese*, and we were then taken to a small gathering of buildings that made up the small military outpost. Having made us welcome, the captain, who was intrigued to hear of our quest for the mitla, showed us to a small, airless room where we deposited our kit-bags and sleeping-rolls. In the late afternoon and evening, the two officers, some of the soldiers, Ilmar and I, sat around the camp fire and, with the help of the smoke, avoided as much of the mosquito life as was possible. As the lieutenant had previously intimated that he was able to understand written English, I produced my correspondence with Brian Fawcett, who had advised me to try to make contact with the Pacahuara Indians in the forest region between the Abuna and the Beni, for they were the people most likely to provide information about the mitla.

When the lieutenant informed the captain of my interest in trying to contact the Pacahuaras, both men became visibly agitated. The lieutenant then went to the captain's quarters from where he returned with a crumpled photograph, which was formally handed to me. To my surprise, the photograph depicted what looked like a teenage youth with arrows embedded in his back, the body having had both of its legs removed. It was, in fact, the body of a Brazilian who had been tapping the wild rubber trees some 50km (30 miles) to the south of the Abuna and that, having encroached on the Pacahuara's territory, he had met his fate. The body had been then conveyed to a nearby landmark, to ensure that it was discovered before it became too decomposed, such an act being intended as a warning to deter all other strangers from venturing into the Indians' hunting grounds.

By now, I was pleased to have the excuse not to travel any further and was especially grateful for this up-to-date information about the Pacahuara's attitude to strangers, for without such a warning, I could have easily blundered into their

midst. By now, I had lost all enthusiasm for exploring the Bolivian forests and as the captain had already learnt from his soldiers that none of them had ever heard the word mitla, nor could they identify any animal they had seen in the surrounding forests as fitting the description provided by Colonel Fawcett, nor were they able to recognise from the identikit tile any animal that they had seen in the forests, I decided that the time had come to retrace our river journey to Abuna.

The return journey was a much easier passage than the journey upstream, for by going into the midstream current, in some places we only had to guide the craft as opposed to doing any strenuous paddling. The most memorable event of the trip took place during one of our midday stops when we disturbed a small family group of silken-haired red howler monkeys. This prompted a large male to start its deep, long-drawn-out roaring, a vocalisation that was soon taken up by the rest of the group. The forest rang first with the sound of a pumping growl, then with a series of booming howls. Once the monkeys had become accustomed to our presence, they concluded their vociferations and as the dapplings of the sun enriched their rust-coloured coats, they stuffed themselves with leaves from the upper and middle storeys of their midday resting site, their prehensile-tails providing a valuable anchor for the acrobatics that they performed from such a height.

The black lion tamarin represents one of the world's rarest primates with an estimated wild population of less than one hundred (Russell A. Mittermeier)

By the time we paddled our way across the confluence of the Abuna with the Madeira and reached Ilmar's home settlement, I recognised that I had not thrown any further light on the question of whether Colonel Fawcett's legendary animal had ever existed or not. Perhaps the mitla had been nothing more than a melanistic form of one of the several species of South American tiger cats or, as has been suggested, the black form of the jaguarundi which can grow to about the size of a foxhound and could, to a non-zoologist, appear to be half-dog, half-cat. Both Senõr Carlos and Professor Gaston Bejarano had confirmed that the black form of the jaguarundi occasionally occurred in the north-eastern regions of Bolivia. However, I had learnt one important fact from my travels in this great integrated region of rivers and forests: that while these remoter areas of the Amazon basin still remain in existence, the forests could well harbour such animals as the mitla that are still strange to science, but it would only be by chance if their presence ever came to light.

Ilmar helped me to collect the rest of my kit from the police station and to convey it to the squalor of the Abuna Hotel. I gave him a fistful of Brazilian notes and as, on leaving his boat, I had already told him that he could keep the remainder of the rations, he appeared to be well satisfied with his reward. When he shook me warmly by the hand, I was surprised at my own emotions in having to say farewell to someone who had shared this most poignant part of life's experience.

At 6.15 on a Tuesday morning, I paid the equivalent of 40p for a ticket to allow me to travel on the Madeira–Mamore Railway, known as the 'Mad Maria' for short, from Abuna to Porto Velho. The EFM–M had had a remarkable history, being known as the 'Railway of Death' or the 'Road of the Devil'. Because there were some twenty-three small rapids between Guajara-Mirim and Porto Velho on the Mamore and Madeira rivers, the railway was built to provide the land-locked Bolivia with access to the sea via the Madeira and the Amazon itself. According to some reports, up to half a million people had died during its construction, but even the most conservative of estimates put the death toll at between ten and thirty-three thousand – a death for every wooden sleeper laid.

In 1867, as part of a friendship treaty between Brazil and Bolivia, it had been agreed to construct a railroad through the dense swampy jungle between Porto Velho and Guajara-Mirim. In 1874, two British companies attempted to make a start, but the majority of their Irish labour force died of beriberi, yellow fever and malaria. However, four years later, an American firm succeeded in constructing 6km (10 miles) of track, which was inaugurated in 1879 prior to an epidemic that forced them to abandon the work. The project then languished until 1903 when because the world market for rubber soared, Bolivia became so desperate to transport its rubber to the navigable Amazon, that it agreed that if Brazil could finish the construction work, then that country could annex the territory known as the Acre. It was at this time and in this area, that Colonel Fawcett was employed to chart the international boundaries concerned.

An American firm was contracted, the majority of whose labour force had worked on the Panama Canal and were accustomed to the privations of such harsh tropical conditions. The railroad was finally inaugurated in 1912, which ironically coincided with the collapse of the South American rubber market. The

railroad had been the most costly on record and, although wild animals and the local Indian tribes were at first expected to be the main threats to its construction, it had soon proved to be the multitude of tropical diseases that had laid claim to the lives of the vast majority of the labour force.

The train takes two days to steam along the single-track line, stopping half way for the night at Abuna, where it conveniently crosses over with its sister train coming from the opposite direction, each train making the journey twice-weekly between the ports of Porto Velho and Guajara-Mirim. At the time of my journey the massive wood-burning locomotive pulled a load of five goods trucks and two passenger carriages, the latter of which were constantly patrolled by three armed, uniformed railway guards, who kept viewing the passengers as if some civil unrest or international crisis was about to erupt at any moment. Although the wooden seats and the stickiness of the atmosphere did little to enhance the mode of transportation, it was a pleasant change not to have to organise such progress oneself.

Although the track kept close to the Rio Madeira, in places it would suddenly turn into the forest to make a short-cut between a bend in the river. On one of these short-cuts, and while the train was attempting to climb a steep gradient, it shuddered to a halt. Ten minutes later, most of the passengers were out on the track and, with the attentiveness of a religious study group, were gazing at the left-side wheels of the first goods truck, which had managed to run off the sunken rails, which looked as if they had been seldom if ever serviced.

After some half-hour of deliberations between a number of peaked-capped

The 'Railway of Death' was built at the time of the rubber-boom days at the beginning of the century to provide landlocked Bolivia with access to the sea via the Rio Madeira and the Amazon itself

Captive Breeding Aiding Species Survival

A 1987 Policy Statement from the International Union for Conservation of Nature and National Resources (IUCN) records: Habitat protection alone is not sufficient if the expressed goal of the World Conservation Strategy, the maintenance of biotic diversity, is to be achieved. Establishments of self-sustaining captive populations and other supportive intervention will be needed to avoid the loss of many species, especially those at high risk in greatly reduced, highly fragmented, and disturbed habitats. Captive breeding programmes need to be established before species are reduced to critically low numbers, and thereafter need to be co-ordinated internationally according to sound biological principles, with a view to the maintaining or re-establishment of viable populations in the wild.

DEPT. OF AGRICULTURE

BRITISH GUIANA Nº A 00890

Veterinary Health Certificate

EXPORT

I hereby certify that I have this day examined at the request of ....

.... *J. J. Mallinson* ....

Address .... *c/o Zoological Park, Botanical Gardens, Georgetown, British Guiana* ....

Description of Animals ...... *one (1) marmoset* ....

.... *one (1) spectacled owl* ....

For export to ...... *Channel Islands – Jersey Zoological Park* ....

to be shipped by .... *Airline* ....

and have found same to be free from evidence of communicable disease.

Patrick McKenzie D.V.M.
Assistant Director (Veterinary.)

Date ...... *6th Dec 1965* ......

C.G.P.6 S. 819/62

MINISTRY OF AGRICULTURE, FORESTS & LANDS,
P.O. Box 256, Georgetown,
British Guiana
26th November, 1965

AGR. 2/40/3V

BRITISH GUIANA

PERMISSION is hereby granted to **Mr. Jeremy J. Mallinson, c/o Jersey Zoological Park, Channel Islands** in terms of Section 7 of the Wild Birds Protection Ordinance, Chapter 260 to collect and export **1 pair Trumpeter Birds and 1 pair Crested Currasows Jersey Wildlife Preservation Trust, Les Augres Manor, Trinity, Jersey Channel Islands.**

Dated this 26th day of November, 1965

Harry Paul.

Chief Agricultural Officer (ag.)

CONDITIONS

1. This licence expires on the **26th day of December, 1965.**
2. The licensee is required to surrender this licence to the Customs Officer when the items named herein have been shipped or at the date of expiration of this licence, whichever date falls first.
3. A certificate of health signed by a Government Veterinary Officer should accompany the shipment.

officials, most of whom had the gold lettering of EFM–M emblazoned across their hat brims, some massive, half-moon shaped pieces of steel were placed to the rear of each set of derailed wheels. The locomotive was then detached from its load and, after emitting a shrill whistle and belching some clouds of charcoal smoke, it advanced about a hundred yards up the gradient. It then stopped and while the armed guards were still motioning to the onlookers to keep well clear of the carriages, the train started to career backwards and suddenly hit the semi-derailed goods truck with all its weight. On impact, the beleaguered left-side wheels of the goods truck almost reached the crown of the steel wedges but just failed to do so, although the engine's large gaping wheels continued to skid unprogressively in its attempt to push the goods truck just a few more inches, with the result that it toppled back onto the now built-up line.

Two Tarzan-like Negroes, stripped to their waists and glistening with perspiration, kept manoeuvring the heavy wedges to a better vantage point, while the locomotive made yet another trip up and down the line; and for a split-second, the derailed wheels almost mounted the zenith of the half-moon wedge, balanced precariously, before they slipped back to the ground again.

A carnival atmosphere prevailed throughout the operation. Each time the train thudded into the goods truck and failed in its attempt to join with it, cheers and laughter greeted the event, the only unenthusiastic noises came from the jets of compressed steam from the engine, for the hotter the locomotive became, the more frequently it allowed such emissions to escape from its massive iron framework. When the engine finally achieved its objective, there was much cheering and handshaking, as if the onlookers had been responsible for putting

The river turtle has a long history of over-exploitation, originally for oil production and more recently as a luxury food for the expanding human population

43

matters right and, as if to provide a climax to such an occasion, one of the guards fired his pistol into the air.

It was during this two-hour unscheduled stop that I came across a goods truck loaded with some seventy specimens of the giant South American river turtle *Podocnemis expansa*, which were locally known as 'tartaruga' for females and 'capitari' for males. It was sad to see the way they had been irreverently piled on top of each other and exposed to the heat of the day without any moisture within their reach. By the time they had reached their destination at Porto Velho, over a quarter of them had died.

There was a considerable trade in river turtles and in places such as Villa Murtinho and Abuna, they fetched the equivalent of 25p each. The Madeira–Mamore railway always carried a large load of tartarugas during the months of June to December, so that, taking into consideration that the trains made two journeys a week from Guajara-Mirim, it could be estimated that between 3,000 and 4,000 turtles were transported during these six months each year. It was not surprising, therefore, that the species was becoming increasingly rare in populated regions and, since it was now considered to be a luxury was ever more in demand.

The demand for such produce as tinned turtle soup in the Western world was not only taking away from the river-dwellers of the Amazon basin an important part of the protein in their staple diet, but was causing the disappearance of a species in all but some of its most remote and unpopulated jungle regions. In Manaus, licences were issued each year, and a fee paid to the local authorities, that permitted holders the control of harvesting turtles over a certain river beach, although the permit stipulated the numbers of turtles that could be marketed and forbade the collection of eggs. INPA hoped that the authorities would enforce a closed season during the egg-laying period by banning the marketing of turtles in order to reverse the current drastic decline in the numbers caused by the over-exploitation of this most beneficial of species.

In 1985, a WWF–US project aimed at investigating interactions between economic development and wildlife populations conducted a case study of the exploitation of turtles in western Brazilian Amazonia. Andrew Johns subsequently reported that the giant South American river turtle has a long history of over-exploitation, originally for oil production and more recently as a luxury food for the expanding human population. Tartaruga barbecues are now something of a status-imparting event among the upper and middle classes, often served to dignatories and visiting politicians. During the time of the study, in the small town of Tefi in the lower River Amazon the average price of a tartaruga, depending on size, ranged from US$40 to 130. Prices in Manaus were two to three times those of Tefi and in southern Brazil prices were higher still.

Although the Brazilian Forestry Development Institute (IBDF) polices tartaruga nesting beaches, they are frequently poached and IBDF lacks the funds necessary to station sufficient guards on these beaches. Anthony Johns highlights that whereas subsistence hunting is a way of life in many parts of the Amazon basin and is impossible, perhaps undèsirable, to prevent, commercial exploitation of turtles could, and should, be curtailed. He concludes: 'Amazon turtles were once so abundant as to be likened to the grains of sand on a beach, but similes rather like this were also applied to passenger pigeons.'

·3·
From River Dolphins to Lion Tamarins

THE trans-Amazonian highway was still several years away from reaching its goal and the Brazilian government had yet to make the city of Manaus a free-trade zone, providing foreign companies with duty free on the component products they imported, which has resulted in a proliferation of high-tech assembly operations with many Japanese electronic companies.

In the mid-1960s, the roads and tracks leading out of Manaus meandered for a time before their eventual disappearance into the oblivion of the surrounding tropical rain forest. It was a city that could not fail to charm the traveller with its crumbling European elegance and its many reflections on its previous grandeur. The massive brown artery of the Rio Negro provides Manaus with its lifeline to the Amazon and its 1,609km (1,000 mile) journey to the Atlantic Ocean. Because of the very deep and slow-moving water, this part of the Rio Negro affords a splendid natural harbour for shipping, which was developed and became in the late nineteenth century a great distributing port and export centre.

The Manaus market was designed by the French architect, Alexandre Eiffel, its ornate iron structure, white marble counters and lofty hallways provide a care-free reminder of the city's former trading importance and reflected glory

By 1887 exports of rubber through Manaus exceeded those of any other state in the Amazon region and, with the invention of the motor car and the pneumatic tyre, the much celebrated boom in the rubber trade took place. The rubber barons created an opulent society and, during the early 1900s, money began to flow like water, champagne bubbled, expensive jewellery sparkled and what has been referred to as an unbridled orgy of spending developed in Manaus, the capital of the world's rubber trade.

Small palaces – colonial mansions amid tree-shaded boulevards – sprang up. The new Opera House, built with choice marbles imported from Italy and windows from the finest Venetian glass, presented performances with the cream of European artistes. The Palace of Justice was built to resemble a miniature Versailles, whereas the Customs House was built entirely of yellowish stone and materials sent from Great Britain, together with the tram-lines and trams that had been manufactured in Cardiff. The waterworks at Manaus had been installed by British engineers at the end of the nineteenth century, and a particularly ornate gold-leafed fountain, situated opposite the Customs House, boasted many nude cherub trumpet players; a small brass plate informed the onlooker that the fountain had been made at the Sun Foundry, Glasgow.

Fortnightly steamers to London, Lisbon and New York maintained the flow of the luxury items required, until between 1910 and 1912, the bubble started to burst, which heralded the city's decline. Rubber trees were stolen and taken to Malaya and arranged in plantations that could yield the latex at a much lower cost, causing rubber prices to drop sharply. Owing to the vast system of unlimited credit, this totally unexpected decline in world prices caused the great commercial houses in Manaus and Belem to be ruined almost overnight.

In spite of the vibrations of wealth and imported culture that had been squandered on this former centre of the world's rubber industry, the city's present inhabitants have inherited the care-free attitude of their forefathers. Even the inhabitants of the rat-infested raft houses situated close to the Manaus market, and those living in wooden hovels on the outskirts of the city, appeared to guide their lives by laughter.

The Manaus market appeared to be the city's terminus of activity with the odour of rotting fish and meat wafting through the ornate iron structure designed by the French architect, Alexandre Eiffel. The white marble counters exhibited steaks of the mermaid-like manatee, enormous catfish, piles of eels and unfriendly-looking piranha. Apart from the multitude of people passing over the cobbled slipway and through the flag-stoned lofty hallways of the meat and fish markets, groups of the common black vulture served as ardent disciples to the merchants, some perching on the ornate ironwork above the stalls, while others stood as great opportunists at the end of the marble slabs, never missing an opportunity to grab some flesh, which sometimes ended up in a tug-o-war between merchant and vulture. If the meat was reclaimed it was hastily returned to the pile of fly-infested flesh for sale.

Having checked with Dr Paul Anthony at INPA about the protective legislation concerning the giant river turtles, I was provided with the opportunity to examine their collection of animal skins which gave an excellent idea of the diversity of the species to be found in the state of Amazonia. I have always been keen on the marmoset and tamarin family of primates (Callitrichidae), so it was of

The pied bare-face tamarin inhabits the vicinity of Manaus on the east bank of the Rio Negro where it used to be abundant, but now due to hunting activities and the clearance of its habitat it has now become a threatened species (Nicholas Lindsay)

particular interest to see museum drawer upon drawer of skins and skeletal material of the pied bare-face tamarin. Owing to the confined distribution of this species, for it inhabits the vicinity of Manaus on the east bank of the Rio Negro to the north bank of the Amazonas, it has now become a threatened species. Despite this, I was offered illegally a pair of pied tamarins for £8.

A small collection of live animals were on display in front of Manaus cathedral, by the children's playground, where southern red-billed whistling ducks, trumpeter birds, parrots, parakeets, squirrel monkeys, capuchin monkeys and a solitary woolly monkey could all be purchased. Just outside the city, situated in Parque 10, a similar assortment of endemic animals could be viewed with groups of capybaras, agoutis and deer adding to the variety of exotics. An animal trader, Augusto Grimaldi, offered me a pair of jaguar for £32, but I informed him that I was not in the business of encouraging such trade.

Manaus very much represented the crossroads of the Amazonas and a number of scientists were carrying out research in the area. A Dr Bernard Lavy, Professor of Botany at Louisiana State University, had made an extensive collection of fungi; Dr Jacques Gery, a Frenchman who had studied gorillas in the Gabon and a team of Americans from the Niagara Falls aquarium were observing nine individuals of the Amazon dolphin and the smaller La Plata River dolphin, which were to be flown shortly to North America.

The dolphins navigated the confines of the large muddy pond with amazing

agility, surfacing every half minute or so to gasp fresh intakes of air. More often than not, they would swim in pairs, carrying out the most exquisite displays in tandem, swivelling in their tracks in order to pick up the fish they had been thrown, one of them being sufficiently tame to take fish given by hand.

Canvas-lined, coffin-shaped boxes had been tailor-made for the transportation of the dolphins. The animals were each to be suspended on a polythene hammock within the boxes, which were to be filled with some 20cm (8in) of water – sufficient to keep the individuals moist and to prevent their delicate skins from being scratched or bruised. It was also intended to provide these most friendly looking of mammals with tranquillisers before and during their journey north.

A recent IUCN-sponsored workshop has drawn attention to the fact that, although the Amazon river dolphins in the Amazon and Orinoco are believed to be in good conditon, they are becoming increasingly vulnerable to the effects of fishing, the development of hydro-electricity, deforestation and pollution. Also, the status of La Plata dolphins is uncertain, but large numbers have been killed in gill-nets throughout its range in Argentina, Uruguay and Brazil over the last thirty years. A rescue operation recently began in central Brazil to save some of the hundreds of Amazon river dolphins that become trapped behind the dams of irrigation channels when the water level recedes. The dolphins are being killed also for their eyes and genital organs, which are sold as lucky charms and aphrodisiacs. The rescue operation is a joint effort by biologists at the University of Minas Gerais and an international team of naturalists, vets and biologists.

The flight from Manaus to Boa Vista appeared to maintain an atmosphere of uncertainty throughout, for soon after taking off it was apparent that one of the port engines was experiencing some difficulties. An American cattle rancher from the Boa Vista region informed me that this was the pilot's maiden flight north of the Amazon, after which I noted that the plane's registration, emblazoned in large letters on the wings, spelt SAD. Once the sickening propeller on the port side had come to a standstill, the pilot complied with the ruling for domestic flights when experiencing mechanical problems, to stick to the course of the river, for if they do have to ditch, they have every chance of being located.

As the plane was well behind schedule, the captain announced that we would be breaking the normal ruling for domestic flights and would have to fly after dusk. It was at this time that the solitary American passenger appeared to take some pleasure in informing me that there were no airport lights on the earthen landing-strip at Boa Vista. Forty minutes later, the dense canopy of the Amazonian tropical rain forest had surrendered to the high savannah lands that surround the Rio Branco delta and the darkness had arrived with its usual tropical suddenness. Unknown to us, two Brazilian-assembled Willy's jeeps had just had time to clear the cattle off the landing-strip and had taken up their stations with their headlights on full in order to guide the plane down safely to earth. Two days later I arrived in British Guiana.

Both the temperature and humidity hovered in the mid-eighties, but the great wooden verandah of Georgetown's Park Hotel, which resembled a massive stage crowned by a dome with an impressive railed gallery above its central portion, was amply fanned by the constant airstream provided by the north-east trade winds. A number of British expatriates reclined comfortably on the Berbice chairs, which derived their names from one of the colony's five rivers, and were characterised by having extended arms enabling the tallest of people to put their feet up and sprawl out over the intricate lattice-canework of their seats.

It had been the Dutch, in 1782, who had moved their seat of colonial government from the Demerara territory down-river to the present site of Georgetown. As the land was 1.2m (4ft) below sea level at high tide, the Dutch utilised their dyking skills by constructing a large sea-wall and a system of streets divided by canals, in the manner of their home country. These canals have been essential for drainage control and smaller drainage channels skirted each street. During the night hours, congregations of tree-frogs maintained a constant chorus and, if you were to close your eyes while sitting on the hotel's verandah or on a bench on the central path of Main Street, one could well have been in the depths of the Okavango swamps or in the midst of the Amazonas. It seemed incongruous to be exposed to such a volume of amphibian vocalisation in the midst of a nation's bustling capital. During the day-time, the role of the singing tree-frogs was usurped by the *qu'est-ce que dit?* calls of the sulphur-yellow breasted shrikes; these starling-sized birds were given their *nom de plume* by the early French settlers because of the bird's magpie-like curiosity.

En route to Georgetown's famous botanical gardens, in which the zoo is situated, the taxi had to pick its way with great adroitness through the multitude of swaying cyclists in Main Street. The gnarled writhing beauty of the saman and flamboyant trees which lined the central path, provided a sombre background to the brilliant whiteness of the painted wooden buildings. The colossal Gothic-styled wooden cathedral overshadowed the main square to the left, whereas Victorian colonial architecture boasted balconies made up of a lace-work of wrought iron, and the building's decorated façades helped to dilute the solemnity of the large white stone statue of Queen Victoria herself.

The botanical gardens cover an area of about 73ha (180 acres) and were veined by pinkish gravel paths and an elaborate system of irrigation and drainage channels. Neatly cut parkland lawns stretched generously between both indigenous and alien plantings. A variety of palm trees thrust their ostrich-like forms into the tropical blue sky, while a stand of towering ubiquitous eucalyptus,

(Overleaf) Manatees have become increasingly threatened throughout their range. Frequently hunted for meat, caught up in nets, subjected to injury by boats and in heavily populated areas affected by both disturbance and pollution, it is hoped that special management areas and new legislation will provide a more secure future for this most amiable group of mammals (Robert Rattner)

49

an extravagantly girthed baobab, intermingled with dense clusters of bamboo and a few of the sharply spiked sand-box trees.

A small family group of manatees inhabited a muddy-complexioned pond close to a large expanse of well-manicured lawns. Although it was possible to observe a lot of movement beneath the water, it was not until the arrival of three Guianese-Indian school-girls that this strangely supple sea-cow could be observed. One of the girls commenced to call up the manatees by taking deep breaths and whistling in and out, while her two companions sprinkled handfuls of grass on the surface of the water. Almost to order, the unhurried movements of the two or three manatees could be seen, their rubber-like muzzles being first to break the surface in order to suck in as much grass as possible. Once the grass on the surface had been cleared, the larger one of the three came half out of the water onto the bank to take further handfuls of grass proffered to them by the girls.

There are, today, two living kinds of sea-cows, the manatees and dugongs; a third kind, the Steller's sea-cow, was exterminated by sealers and whalers in the northern Pacific at the end of the eighteenth century. Since time immemorial, these curious aquatic milk-giving beasts were purported to have been the origin of the legendary mermaid, on account of the manatee's habit of standing straight up in the water with head and shoulders above the surface, the females often holding nursing infants with one crooked fore-flipper to their rather prominent breasts. Manatees are cow-sized mammals inhabiting the Atlantic coasts of the Americas from Florida around the Caribbean to the Orinoco, the Guianese and the Amazonian river mouths; they survive in salt, brackish or freshwater lagoons, and in the smaller river mouths almost everywhere about those regions. Its forelegs are flippers without digits, and instead of hindlegs it has a large horizontal tail-fin which acts as a circular paddle. The small eyes on its head are dramatically dominated by a sensitive muzzle; the nostrils act as valves, closing when the animal submerges.

Manatees were once abundant, but now have become increasingly threatened throughout their range. In spite of a degree of legal protection, manatees are frequently hunted for meat, caught up in nets and are, in heavily populated areas, becoming increasingly struck by boats and injured. It is hoped that special management areas and new legislation will provide a more secure future for this most distinctly amiable group of mammals.

Guiana's National Zoo is now starting to specialise in exhibiting South American fauna, chiefly those forms of wildlife that inhabited the area between the Orinoco and the Amazon regions. A five-year development programme had commenced three years previously, and on its completion it was intended to establish a wildlife survival centre that concentrated on indigenous fauna. Giant ant-eaters, peccaries, capybaras, brocket deer, sloths, harpy eagles, trumpeter birds, currasows, caiman and anacondas, all well illustrated to the local people the great diversity and wealth of Guiana's wildlife heritage.

While viewing the sounder of some sixteen white-lipped peccaries, the zoo's superintendent, Stanley Lee, suggested that I should take back a small collection of Guianese animals to the British Isles. Although a small breeding population of the smaller collared peccary had been established in Jersey, this attractive white-moustached and reddish-brown coated species was not found in northern European zoos. Whereas little work had been carried out at that time on either of the two known species, a third peccary form was only discovered in the wild in 1972. Having been known previously only from fossils, the Chacoan peccary is mainly concentrated in the Chaco Boreal region of Paraguay. However, despite the attempt by conservationists to excite public interest in the ecology and conservation of the entire Chaco basin area, this rediscovered third form of peccary now appears to be on its way to extinction owing to the destruction of its habitat and hunting.

On my return to the Park Hotel, I cabled both the US and British licensing authorities to enquire whether I would be allowed to ship six white-lipped peccaries via New York to the United Kingdom. Some thirty hours later, I took delivery of two very long telegrams, both emphatically refusing my request on account of the stringent quarantine restrictions on all movements of the pig family to prevent any of the transmittable diseases being spread to the pig industry on both sides of the Atlantic.

Undeterred by the refusal, I was still enthusiastic to return to the British Isles with at least a few species of Guiana's exotic fauna. With only two weeks left in order to accumulate a small collection, I was tempted to obtain a cross-section of species that were readily available. A pair of the magnificent jungle-inhabiting harpy eagles was surplus to the zoo's requirements, but I realised that we should not be able to accommodate such a large and powerful crested raptor satisfactorily. I had seen a great number of pelts of the giant otter in Bolivia and Brazil, but in Guiana it was reported to live unmolested in creeks and flood plains along the

The white-lipped peccary the largest of the three known forms goes about in large droves and due to its sizeable distribution is at present in no way threatened. However, its close relative the Chacoan peccary, from Paraguay, now appears to be on its way to extinction owing to hunting and destruction of known habitat

The Royal Animal of the Incas

In the chill uplands of the Central Andes at altitudes of from 12-18,000ft a small kind of llama, the vicuna, wanders about in small family parties. Although it has never been successfully domesticated it has, until comparatively recently, been hunted for its exceptionally fine fleece that falls in a pendent bundle from the base of the neck of the males.

The whole pelt of the vicuna is exceptionally soft and silky and both fleece and hide were originally reserved for the Incan rulers and their entourage. After the arrival of the Europeans the animal was nearly exterminated, for vicuna wool is of incomparable quality and the fabric derived from it represents the most luxuriant and valuable of all wool products.

In 1957, the vicuna population was estimated at approximately 400,000 individuals of which about a quarter of a million inhabited Peru. In 1972, the numbers in Peru had fallen to about 15,000. This relentless commercialised poaching arose from international demand for vicuna wool and skins, notably from the United States and Great Britain. Prior to a ban on all such imports, one British manufacturer alone imported two to three tons of vicuna wool a year, equivalent to the yield from about 4,000 animals, all of which would have been killed. In the time of the Incas, hunting was conducted on rational game management lines that permitted a 'crop' to be harvested without impairing the basic stocks.

With increased human activities encroaching deeper into the Andes, the vicuna has been obliged to retreat to the higher and more remote areas. However, conservationists recognise that the vicuna represents a classic example of a wild animal occupying a highly specialised ecological niche where it is not in competition with man. For it possesses the useful attribute of being capable of thriving on the sparse high altitude vegetation of the *puna* and of converting it into wool and meat of superlative quality. It has therefore been established that the protection of the vicuna is the wisest, as well as the most rewarding form of land-use, to which the *puna* zone can be put. It is also self-evident that under a properly regulated management system the vicuna could make a significant contribution to rural economies.

Successful experiments in vicuna capture and shearing has been recently carried out, which has resulted in 3,500kg (700lb) of wool in stock in Peru. Also, with the successful translocation of more than 2,000 animals, it is hoped that local people may soon begin to benefit more from the presence of vicuna on their lands; especially when the international conservation community manage to arrive at a satisfactory solution to the complex situation whereby vicuna cloth, sheared from the vicuna and woven in Peru, will eventually be legally on sale again. (Photo: Marwell Preservation Trust)

coast. It had been a wonderful sight to watch a pair of these incredible animals, the largest of all otters, which can grow to over 1.8m (6ft) in length, humping over the muddy banks of their enclosure on their bellies, feasting on river mussels and then returning to the water to continue their seal-like characteristics of standing upright in the water and barking. Their constant activity and curiosity would have made them an excellent exhibit at any European zoo, but tailor-made accommodation would have been essential.

I almost accepted the gift of a pair of grey-black giant ant-eaters from the population of eight at the zoo, because the species represented perhaps the most streamlined of all mammals living in South America, with their icicle-shaped heads and enormous bushy tails. I also had to decline a pair of the world's largest rodents, the capybara. However the small collection that I was soon to leave the Atkinson airfield with comprised an interesting assortment of mammals, birds and reptiles, which included the two-toed sloth, red-handed tamarin, grey-winged trumpeter bird, spectacled owl, crested curasow, teguexin lizard and anaconda. Some of these species, such as the sloths and the curasows, were to be new to the Jersey collection, whereas the majority were to provide unrelated pairings to individuals both in Jersey and elsewhere within the British Isles.

Before leaving Guiana, I took a Transport of Harbours Department Steamers ticket to Adventure. It had been during 1950 that Gerald Durrell had first visited British Guiana to collect animals for various zoological gardens in the United Kingdom and Ireland, and, fifteen years after his visit, I retraced his steps from Georgetown to the other bank of the Demerara, then to the Parika train which conveyed its passengers erratically to the ferry that travelled to the west bank of the Essequibo river.

The ornithological pageant that Gerald had described embracing dozens of military starlings, snowy egrets, jacanas, marsh birds and snail hawks were all very much in abundance, confirming that the environment he had described as a landscape seemingly overloaded with birds had been left unaltered. Even the small stone jetty and the corrugated iron roof of the shed, with the bold printed white letters announcing to the outside world that the small trading landing place was indeed Adventure, had been left unchanged in this backwater of human activity.

As the jet provided its inter-continental passengers with an albatross' lofty view over the azure-blue waters of the Caribbean studded with atolls and islands, I recognised that exposure to the irresistible fascinations of the natural history of the Amazon network of rivers, had been both beneficial and rewarding. Although I was returning to my home base to help Gerald Durrell with the development of his newly formed Jersey Wildlife Preservation Trust, I reassured myself that it would not be too long before I returned to this continent of natural history treasures for few detailed field studies had at that time been carried out on South America's indigenous fauna.

The Atlantic forest region of eastern Brazil is already endangered, and unhappily, this very region embraces the last homelands of some thirteen species of primates, including the three forms of lion tamarins: the golden lion tamarin, the golden-headed lion tamarin and the golden-rumped, or black lion, tamarin. All three species are classified in the IUCN Red List of Threatened Animals as endangered,

Spectacled owl
(Evening Post Jersey)

which covers those species in danger of extinction in the wild and whose survival is unlikely if the causal factors continue operating.

It was not until the first half of the 1960s that the doyen of Brazil's present-day primatologists, Dr Adelmar Coimbra-Filho, called attention to the severe plight of the golden lion tamarin and some measures were adopted in order to prevent further devastation of the remnant populations. In 1970, Dr Coimbra-Filho rediscovered the golden-rumped species after it had not been seen for a period of sixty-five years; until the late 1970s it had never been kept in captivity. In 1972, the golden-headed species had only been in captivity on three occasions: in London in 1869, once in Rio de Janeiro in 1961 and then from 1971 with Dr Coimbra-Filho.

It is regrettable that the remaining forest for their restricted distribution, estimated at less than 2 per cent of their original available habitat, is within the most densely inhabited and developed region of Brazil. Deforestation for lumber, agriculture, pasture, recreation and housing, are the chief dangers to the ultimate chances of survival of the remnant wild populations of the three forms of

Leontopithecus. With such a decline in recent years of all three species, it was evident that, unless dramatic changes occurred to reverse the inroads into the remaining pockets of good, fresh habitat, the lion tamarins could well become extinct in the wild by the year 2000.

With the wild population so threatened, captive breeding of the tamarins became a crucial factor for the animals' survival. With this in mind, a Wild Animal Propagation Trust was formed in the USA which began to monitor the captive population of golden lions. In 1972, the Propagation Trust organised an international conference to save the golden lion. At that time, the outlook for the captive population was poor and it seemed likely that it would become extinct within a decade. However, optimists felt that the exchange of information and publicity provided by the conference might be a turning point. And so it proved, and much of the subsequent success of what is now an international co-operative breeding programme is due to the professional wisdom and enthusiastic motivation of Dr Devra Kleiman, Assistant Director for Research at the Smithsonian Institution's National Zoological Park, Washington, DC.

As holder of the international stud-book for the golden lion tamarins since 1976, Dr Kleiman has co-ordinated the co-operative captive breeding programme that has brought the captive population from some seventy individuals in 1972, to more than five hundred today. The conservation programme for the golden lion includes, in addition to captive propagation, field studies of behavioural ecology, habitat protection and restoration, public and professional education, and the introduction and reintroduction of captive-bred animals.

I presented my first paper about the Trust's experience of breeding a number of marmoset and tamarin species in captivity at the time of the First World Conference on the Breeding of Endangered Species. The conference was sponsored jointly by the Jersey Trust and the Fauna Preservation Society and was held in Jersey in May 1972. In 1975, I was asked by Dr Kleiman to present our findings at a conference she had organised in Virginia on the biology and conservation of the Callitrichidae covering all species of the marmoset and tamarin family. Over fifty scientists participated and our collective findings helped to establish more firmly the basic management requirements. Marmoset workshops held at Gottingen University in 1977 and at the University of Bielefeld, West Germany, in October 1984, at which I had been requested to present papers, all helped to guide the conservation community on how best to ensure the maintenance of self-sustaining captive populations, as well as the survival of remnant wild populations.

It was not until March 1983 that I had the opportunity to make the two-hour journey to the Rio de Janeiro Primate Centre, as a guest of its founder and director, Dr Coimbra-Filho. The centre is situated some 100km (62 miles) to the north-east of Rio de Janeiro, and although some parts of the region still boast patches of mature forest, most of the habitat on either side of the road clearly showed the disastrous effects of the slash and burn policy of the local people, with hills revealing the brick-red terminal wounds of soil erosion. The centre is fortunately still embraced by a bank of tropical rain forest, the hills behind forming a dramatic back-drop, representing a permanent reminder of the need to preserve such an oasis of forest for the future not only of the animal kingdom but also of mankind.

In 1983, the centre had some 130 animals belonging to ten different species of Callitrichidae. This treasure chest of diminutive New World primates included all three forms of the lion tamarins. The golden-headed tamarin on display had a wealth of golden fur surrounding its face and shoulders, and the vivid gold of its arms, feet and on the dorsal of its tail, all contrasted magnificently with the jet-black fur of the remainder of its body. The buffy-headed marmoset and its close relative, the buffy-tufted-ear species, were also on show, as well as the more familiar Geoffroy's marmoset, and some live pied tamarins that had been sent to the centre from Manaus.

During this period in Brazil, I visited the Poco das Antas Reserve, which represented a patchwork of primary and secondary forest and pastureland. It was here that field studies on the major remnant of the wild population of the golden lion tamarin had been initiated, involving a major protection and restoration effort of the biological reserve. It was in this protected region that just over a year later, the first reintroduction trials took place with other scientists from the Smithsonian team – Dr Jim Dietz, Lou-Ann Dietz and Dr Ben Beck – who were all working towards the success of this new approach to conservation.

Since the latter part of 1984, I found myself directly involved with a recovery and management programme for the golden-headed lion tamarin. Because a great number of these animals have been exported illegally from Brazil, in March 1985 I was requested by the Brazilian government's IBDF to form an international recovery and management committee. Acting as a technical adviser and consultant to IBDF, the committee has aided the repatriation of some twenty-eight individuals to Brazil, from animal dealers in both Belgium and Japan, as well as returning the ownership to the IBDF of a further twenty-one specimens from

The first golden-headed lion tamarin to be born in North America (Brookfield, Chicago) as part of a co-operative breeding programme for this little known New World primate (Vince Sodaro)

France, Belgium, Hong Kong, Portugal and French Guiana. The committee has met four times, in San Diego, Gottingen and twice in Brasilia, and, apart from having developed a stud-book for the captive population and managing the animals scientifically as a co-ordinated, co-operative breeding programme, the committee represents what is considered to be the only international body that is co-ordinating the management of an endangered species with all the animals and their progeny owned by the country where the species is endemic.

In November 1986, a number of scientists who had been directly involved with conservation measures for both the golden lion tamarin and the golden-headed species, were requested by Dr Faical Simon, chairman of the newly formed international committee for the preservation and management of the black lion tamarin, to serve on his committee. With an estimated wild population of less than one hundred, this form of lion tamarin represents perhaps the world's rarest primate. It is hoped that, because of the great success of the management plan for preservation of the golden lion tamarin, which has now undoubtedly ensured the species' survival, it will not be too long before a multi-disciplinary approach to long-term conservation measures will result in similar success.

During the course of the last decade, the Jersey Wildlife Preservation Trust and its sister organisation, Wildlife Preservation Trust International, have increasingly adopted a multi-faceted approach to its long-term conservation objectives. To date, the combined trusts have invested over US$100,000 in support of significant projects that relate to the conservation of the lion tamarin group. Apart from having developed some viable breeding populations of both

The establishment of a secure captive population of the golden lion tamarin has led to a high profile introduction/re-introduction programme which has acted as powerful political and educational tools promoting support for broader conservation efforts (Russell A. Mittermeier)

the golden lion and the golden-headed tamarin at the Trust in Jersey, we have also helped by aiding conservation education to increase public awareness and support of conservation efforts; assisted in training people in order to develop more effective captive management programmes; taken an active role in supporting reintroduction programmes for the golden lion species and adopting a long-term commitment to such endeavours; helped finance the construction of thirty units of accommodation at the Rio de Janeiro Primate Centre; undertaken a comprehensive survey of the distribution of the golden-headed lion tamarin; as well as helping to co-ordinate the recovery programme of the golden-headed form, and subsequently participated in all three of the international committees for the preservation of this most diverse and stunningly attractive family of golden lions.

In the autumn of 1986, I returned to the Poco das Antas Reserve with the team of Smithsonian and Brazilian scientists that have all contributed so much to aiding the long-term survival of the golden lion tamarin. It soon became clear that the establishment of secure captive populations under international management, introduction/reintroduction programmes can result in 'flagship' species gaining considerable public attention and subsequent increase in support for broader conservation efforts. In the case of the golden lion tamarin, saving sufficient contiguous habitat for the species has in turn aided the conservation of thousands of other species.

·4·
Expedition du Fleuve Zaire

THE Zaire river represents the seventh longest river in the world. From the source near the Zambian border, it runs 4,374km (2,718 miles) to the Atlantic, meandering across the equator twice and discharging into the sea a volume of fresh water, visible on the surface for some 483km (300 miles), which is second only to the Amazon. Its flow is unusually even, for there is always heavy rain over its feeders both to the north and south of the equator. Starting at its head – the source of the River Lualaba – the Zaire river includes numerous unnavigated stretches because of the long and dangerous rapids, some of them up to 161km (100 miles) long, that interrupt its journey to the sea. So 'Fleuve Zaire' sponges the vast amount of water from its equatorial forest basin and squeezes it through the swamps and dense jungle, down cataract and rapid, past places unexplored and unnavigated, until it achieves its relentless ambition of marrying its muddy-complexioned water with those of the Atlantic Ocean.

The Zaire river includes numerous unnavigated stretches because of the long and dangerous rapids, some of them up to 100 miles long, that interrupt its journey to the sea

Henry Morton Stanley had started his river journey, in his beloved *Lady Alice,* approximately 965km (600 miles) below the source of the Lualaba. Because of the hostilities that his eleven-month journey encountered, his team could accomplish relatively little scientific work, for in those days survival was the chief objective. Now, one hundred years later, John Blashford-Snell, the leader of *Expedition du Fleuve Zaire,* in order to keep expedition members on their toes, reminded us, somewhat sardonically, that only 115 out of the 350 in Stanley's expedition reached the end of the river, for sixty-nine had died of smallpox, dysentery and 'terror' (whatever that meant); fifty-eight from 'battle and murder'; eight from starvation; fourteen from drowning; one from smoking hemp; one was lost in jungle; one was caught by crocodile, and fifteen went missing.

Many of the 155 and 10 women who had been selected to join the expedition from nations that included Australia, Belgium, Canada, Denmark, Fiji, Finland, France, Great Britain, Holland, Nepal, New Zealand, the USA and Zaire were members of the Scientific Exploration Society. John B.-S., or 'Blashers', as he was fondly referred to, was chairman of the society and had been planning the expedition since 1971, for it had always been his ambition that the river journey should take place exactly one hundred years after H.M. Stanley had made his famous descent of the Zaire river, formerly known as the Congo, in 1874.

The scientific programme of the Zaire River Expedition had been designed to concentrate on natural, human and medical studies. It included research into tropical eye diseases – onchocerciasis, commonly known as 'river blindness', and bilharzia – and veterinary studies for animal husbandry and wildlife conservation. The general archaeology, freshwater biology, botany, geography, sociology and zoology were to be studied by scientists of all disciplines. I had been accepted as a member of the scientific arm of the expedition to carry out general wildlife studies in eastern Zaire and, provided I was able to arrange it personally, to do some fieldwork on either the mountain or eastern lowland gorilla in Kivu Province.

I had first become fascinated by the gorilla genus some fifteen years previously, when Gerald Durrell had acquired an eighteen-month-old lowland gorilla known as N'Pongo, in 1959. Since that time, I had helped in the rearing of N'Pongo to adulthood, had made a study of the maintenance and breeding of the species in captivity, and was also working towards the development of breeding programmes for gorillas both in the British Isles and on an international basis. It had always been my hope that self-sustaining breeding programmes could be established, which would negate the necessity of taking further specimens from the wild. In Jersey, we had already recorded two successful births in 1973 and a third parturition was expected within the next two months. What I found particularly stimulating was that, whatever was now being recorded and established about one of our closest relatives, it was new to science, for the gorilla species had only as recently as December 1956 first successfully bred in captivity, and multi-generation captive births had only just been recorded.

It was Dr von Hermes, Director of the Berlin Aquarium, who described the first male gorilla to be exhibited in captivity. In 1876 he wrote: 'It seems as if he was born with a patent of nobility among apes . . . In comparison to a chimpanzee, holds his head higher, producing the impression that he belongs to a better class of society.' The gorilla species inhabit the dense moist forests of equatorial Africa. The western lowland gorillas live in the rain forests of the Gulf of Guinea and are

found in the Congo Republic, equatorial Guinea, Gabon, the Cameroons, the extreme south-west of the Central African Republic and south-eastern Nigeria. The eastern lowland and mountain gorillas occur 1,300–1,600km (800–1,000 miles) to the east, in eastern Zaire and over the borders into Rwanda and Uganda.

Of the several kinds of primate that have been known to mankind for upwards of three thousand years, it is extremely doubtful that any of the four existing types of anthropoid – the gibbon, orang-utan, gorilla and chimpanzee – was among those forms that were so well attested by such historical evidence. However, of the four types, the gorilla was the last to be discovered for science; the orang-utan was first properly described in the mid-seventeenth century, and the first evidence of the existence of the gorilla to reach Europe was almost two hundred years later.

Letters from Dr Thomas S. Savage to Richard Owen and Samuel Stutchbury (Curator of the Museum of the British Institution for the Advancement of Science, Literature and the Arts) appear to be the first to record such evidence. A letter dated 24 April 1847 was written by Dr Savage when he stopped over at the Protestant Mission House on the Gaboon river, West Africa, while he was en route to the United States. The letter stated:

I have found the existence of an animal of an extraordinary character in this locality, and which I have reason to believe is unknown to the naturalist. As yet, I have been unable to obtain more than a part of a skeleton.

Female lowland gorillas N'Pongo and Nandi born Cameroons, arrived Jersey 1959, and 1961, have given birth to fourteen infants with grandchildren in Great Britain, Switzerland and the USA (Phillip Coffey)

A captain of a ship trading between the west coast of Africa and Bristol, Captain George Wagstaff, obtained three skulls from the Gaboon river in December 1847. These were presented to Mr Stutchbury and formed the basis of the descriptions that were subsequently published by Richard Owen in 1848.

Seven years later, in 1855, the first live gorilla arrived in Europe, and this young female was exhibited by Wombwell's Travelling Menagerie during the winter of 1855–6 in the Liverpool area of England. Although it was thought at first to be a chimpanzee, it was only later recognised for the then almost unknown species of ape.

In 1861, the explorer Paul du Chaillu wrote that it was his fortune to be the first white man to witness gorillas in darkest Africa. He stated: 'I can vouch that no description can exceed the horror of its appearance, the ferocity of its attack or the impish malignity of its nature.' So the gorilla's maligned character was in the forefront of people's minds at the time the second live specimen arrived in Europe, some twenty years after the first, in 1876. This young male, which was given the name Pongo and was described by Dr von Hermes, went via Liverpool to the Berlin Aquarium but, like the Wombwells' gorilla, only survived in captivity for a short time and died in November 1877. In 1883, the Berlin Aquarium acquired another young gorilla, but this too soon succumbed to the captive conditions of the day.

Between 1887 and 1908, seven young gorillas, two males and five females, were exhibited at the Zoological Society of London, but none of them survived for

The three forms of gorilla – western lowland, eastern lowland, mountain – have a discontinuous distribution from the equatorial forests of West Africa to the montane rain forests of East Central Africa (Tom Hustler)

In 1956 the landmark of a gorilla first breeding successfully in captivity was achieved. By 1988, 50% of both the North American and Great Britain gorilla populations were captive born (Phillip Coffey)

Plunder of the Lion Tamarins

Tropical rain forests contain a major portion of the planet's biological diversity and some of these, such as the Atlantic forest region of Eastern Brazil, are themselves already endangered. Unhappily, this region embraces the last homelands of diverse members of the animal kingdom, amongst which some thirteen species of primates are now endangered. Three of these belong to the somewhat bizarre but dramatic lion tamarin group which consist of three forms: the golden lion tamarin *(Leontopithecus rosalia)*, the golden-headed lion tamarin *(Leontopithecus chrysomelas)*, and the golden-rumped or black lion tamarin *(Leontopithecus chrysopygus)*.

It was not until the first half of the 1960s that attention was called to the severe plight of the golden lion species, and some measures were adopted to prevent further devastation of the remnant populations. In 1970, the black lion tamarin was re-discovered after it had not been seen for a period of sixty-five years; until the late 1970s it had never been kept in captivity. In 1972, the golden-headed species had only been recorded in captivity on three occasions: once at London Zoo in 1869, once in Rio de Janeiro in 1961, and from 1971 it has been maintained by the doyen of Brazil's present day primatologists, Dr Adelmar F. Coimbra-Filho.

Thanks to the successful development of a scientifically co-ordinated and managed captive breeding programme, with research efforts by many individuals and institutions, both in Brazil and elsewhere, the future of the golden lion tamarin has now been ensured. The National Zoological Park, Washington, D.C. figures prominently in this long-term international conservation programme which includes: captive propagation, field studies of behavioural ecology, habitat protection and restoration, public and professional education, and reintroduction of captive-bred animals.

With such a fine model to emulate, it is hoped that similar successes will be achieved by the international conservation community and management committees, for the other two forms of lion tamarins; for at the present the black lion tamarin represents Brazil's most critically endangered primate.

more than a few months. In 1897, a young male with the name of Pussi was exhibited at Breslau Zoological Gardens, Germany, and was maintained there for the then outstanding period of seven years, until it died in October 1904. C.V.A. Peel described seeing Pussi at Breslau, writing in 1903:

> But the animal for which this garden is justly famous is the huge black-faced ape, known as the gorilla from West Africa, the only known specimen in captivity in the world. The ape is housed in a large lofty case with glass front in the monkey house.

The first live gorilla in the United States arrived at Boston in 1897, but lived for only a few days. Fourteen years later, in 1911, the second living gorilla arrived in America, but this, too, soon died.

During a fifty-six year period (1855–1911), only fourteen gorillas were exhibited in Europe and the United States of America and, apart from Pussi, all had died within a comparatively short period of time. Such a lamentable record of events prompted W.T. Hornaday, Director of the New York Zoological Society, to state in 1915:

> There is not the slightest reason to hope that an adult gorilla, either male or female, ever will be seen living in a zoological park or garden . . . It is unfortunate that the ape that, in some respects, stands nearest to man, never can be seen in adult state in zoological gardens; but we may as well accept that fact – because we cannot do otherwise.

A male Sumatran orang-utan, one of the two sub-species who are restricted to Borneo and Sumatra and represent the most arboreal and less sociable of all the anthropoid apes, which include gibbons, gorillas and chimpanzees (Phillip Coffey)

Fortunately, over the years, we have seen how the standard of management of gorillas in captivity has improved, with far better accommodation, nutrition and human involvement; the conventional bar-fronted cage has given way to laminated glass, and with the consequent protection from human germs, gorillas are now living in captivity for a much more acceptable period of time. However, a century after the first gorilla had been exhibited before the public, a number of authorities were still saying that the gorilla was one species that would never successfully reproduce in captive conditions. Happily, such pessimism was subsequently proved to be unfounded for, in December 1956, the landmark of a gorilla breeding successfully in captivity was achieved with the birth of a female infant, Colo, at the St Columbus Zoo, USA. The next two births occurred in Europe at the Basel Zoo, Switzerland; the female Goma in 1959 and the male

Jambo in 1961. Jambo, who soon matured into a proven breeding male, was brought to Jersey by Dr Ernst Lang, at that time one of Europe's most respected zoo directors, and the females N'Pongo and Nandi had already celebrated their union with Jambo by presenting him with viable progeny.

Only comparatively recently have conservationists working in the international zoo world recognised that, if an animal species is going to flourish in a captive environment, it is of vital importance to have knowledge of the life-style in the wild, so that proper provision can be made for better physical and social captive conditions; also, that the long-term future of animal species in captivity as a whole increasingly relies upon national and international co-operation and co-ordination. In the final analysis, recipes for survival can only materialise if the necessary ingredients of professional zoo personnel, field-workers, conservationists, educationalists, academics and others genuinely interested in animal conservation, are willing to co-operate whole-heartedly.

On 2 October, a special service of holy communion was held at St John's Church at Leytonstone for the Zaire River Expedition. It was at this same church that Livingstone took communion before embarking on his last African journey. Basil Pratt, the chaplain to the expedition, presented to all the expedition participants, on behalf of the Naval, Military and Air Force Bible Society, a specially produced revised standard version of the New Testament and psalms. With both the historical and religious elements of the expedition now accounted for, the scene was set for the expedition's departure. Assembling at Gatwick Airport at 5.30am, over a hundred army personnel, scientists, students and explorers, with 20 tons of stores, awaited the departure. Two hours later, a chartered Air Zaire DC 10, with President Mobutu's personal pilot at the controls, made an effortless take-off and climbed like a powerful bird of prey through the bleak, grey clouds of an English October morning.

During the flight, Sinclair Dunnett gave me an inscribed copy of his excellent booklet on a field study that he had carried out with another researcher a few years previously, on two groups of chimpanzee in west and south Guinea. Sinclair explained that he had joined the expedition to attempt to gain access into a remote area on the western side of the upper regions of the Lualaba river, where the pygmy chimpanzee or bonobo was believed to live. As he knew of my fascination for primates, and in particular for anthropoid apes, he asked whether I would care to join him on his proposed journey up one of the lesser tributaries – La Fleuve Lomami. It was an extremely tempting offer, but as my time on the expedition was restricted to under three months, and with my particular goal of carrying out some field observations on the gorilla species, I had to decline.

At Kinshasa, the capital city of the Republic of Zaire, where we eventually touched down, a few of our members were left behind to form the expedition's base there, while a few more people were picked up to join the participants' onward journey of approximately 1,600km (1,000 miles) down to Lubumbashi, situated in the far south-east of the country. At Lubumbashi, we were met by a convoy of army vehicles and received an official welcome from a handful of government officials, who all displayed the red freedom torch of their political overlord. The brief speeches were followed by a somewhat evocative display of tribal dancing by some beautiful Shaba maidens, after which we were given the green light to man-handle our personal belongings to nearby trucks and clamber

aboard for a drive of over 320km (200 miles) to the copper-mining township of *Start of white water*
Kolwezi.

Accompanied by a liaison officer of the Zaire army, the convoy of motley army vehicles, which seemed to range in vintage from veterans of World War II through to the Congo post-independence fighting and to the present time, lumbered its way forward. Twenty minutes later, the lorry that I was riding in stuttered to a standstill and a generous blanket of dust enveloped everyone. Darkness had already arrived with tropical suddenness and, as the dust settled, the first intoxicating smells of the African bush wafted our way.

The shortcomings of the truck in which a section of the scientists had been riding caused the rest of the convoy to come to an uncomfortable halt. Soon, appearing out of the darkness, strode J. B.-S. and, after greeting me, turned his attention to the truck driver and frowned fiercely at the offending engine, which appeared spontaneously to jump into life. It was obvious to all present that our leader had no intention of allowing the expedition to grind to a halt within its first few hours, before it had reached its first field-base.

We arrived late at night at the sprawling township of Kolwezi. In spite of the lateness of the hour, it seemed that most of the African population was there to greet us. As the scientists decanted from the trucks in their paramilitary-type clothing, the Africans took it as their cue to burst into song.

At this stage of the expedition, a Major Ashley Barker had been appointed as the scientific co-ordinator and, as such, he was responsible for our party's welfare. After we had managed to locate our respective kit-bags, a party of about twelve was driven in two Land-Rovers to accommodation that was known as 'Victor Forest's Flats', which was situated above a deserted block of shops. From the state of the place, it looked as if it had not been inhabited since the time of the catastrophes that had swamped and overtaken these regions just after the Congo had been granted its independence by Belgium in the early 1960s. The floor was covered with a carpet of dust; as there was no electricity, two paraffin storm-lamps were

An Avon Professional Vanguard is launched on the Lualaba one hundred years after H.M. Stanley made his famous descent of the Congo River in 1874 (Richard Le Boutillier)

primed and lit; the more the flat was illuminated the less appealing the thought of sleeping under its roof appeared. Ashley Barker, for a fleeting moment, considered that it would be a good idea to start cleaning the place but, sensing a mutiny, he capitulated and allowed his team of scientists to spread out their ground-sheets over the dust residue and collapse, like overladen camels, with their belongings – they had, after all, been travelling for over twenty-four hours.

Before arriving at Kolwezi, I had not realised that there would be a considerable delay of weeks prior to the main part of the expedition, with the three giant inflatables, *La Vision, David Gestetner* and *Barclays Bank,* and the many tons of stores that were ready to move up to Bukama, where they could be launched on their long journey to the Atlantic Ocean.

The main flotilla of the expedition was scheduled to be launched at Bukama, but beforehand, it had been planned to launch the Avon Professionals into the Lualaba near Mumuna, 24km (15 miles) or so from its source, which was situated some 160km (100 miles) across rugged earthen roads from Kolwezi. The boats were expected to encounter a great deal of white water in exceptionally difficult conditions. Fortunately, apart from a palaeontologist, Dr Alan Bartram, who wanted to collect fish from near the Lualaba's source, there was no room in the Avon Professionals for anybody but the white-water experts. With my personal time at such a premium, I decided to ask for leave of absence from the river expedition in order to take advantage of my various contacts and introductions that would hopefully make it possible for me to travel north to Kivu Province, to study the remnant populations of the gorilla kingdom.

·5·

En Route to Gorilla Country

IT WAS a further twenty-four hours before I was able to gain a document from both the police and their military overlords that granted the necessary permission for me to stray away from the jurisdiction of the expedition itself and to travel north to Kivu Province.

Fortunately, some two months prior to embarking on the expedition, I had had the opportunity to show around the Jersey Trust, the wife of the managing director of the Belgian company Amiza which was reputed to be the largest general trading company in Zaire. Furnished with a generous letter of introduction from her husband, I was able to receive a number of favours that otherwise would not have been available to me.

Paul du Nyn was the manager of the Amiza office in Kolwezi and he immediately reacted to the letter of introduction with great enthusiasm. Wireless messages went to and fro between Kolwezi and Lubumbashi until it was arranged that I should be given a lift to Lubumbashi that same afternoon and that I could be accommodated at the Amiza compound. At 1.45pm, I returned to Paul du Nyn's office in civilian clothes, with my well-travelled and seasoned kit-bag on my back. The latter still had the trappings of my Bolivian and Brazilian river journey of some eight years previously, but in order to bring the events recorded on it more up to date, I had taken the precaution of having sewn on it, in a prominent position, the *Expedition du Fleuve Zaire* cloth badge with President Mobutu's freedom torch emblazoned on it. This I considered would do more than anything else to deter the local population from stealing it, for Citizen-President Mobutu, Founder of the Popular Movement for the Revolution, and his political empire, were undoubtedly the masters, even in this once divided and separatist province of Katanga/Shaba.

Just before we were due to depart, and I had already loaded my kit-bag into the boot of a diesel Mercedes 504, a message came through from Lubumbashi stating that it had been impossible to acquire a plane ticket for me to travel Lubumbashi–Bukavu that week, and could I therefore postpone my journey to Lubumbashi for six to seven days. As I had now set my mind on reaching my goal of Bukavu in a few days' time, I told Paul du Nyn that it was imperative that I should now commence my travels and without more ado climbed into the car.

The four-hour journey back to Lubumbashi was far more comfortable than the truck journey of two and half days previously. On one occasion, my driver was

Expedition du Fleuve Zaire cloth badge

71

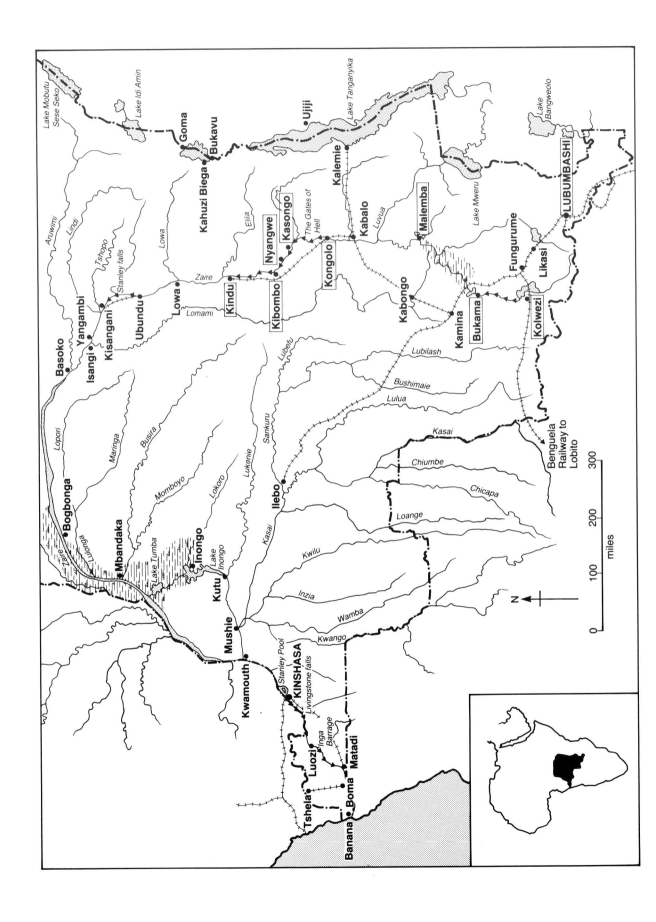

flagged down by an oncoming company car, out of which alighted two well-built Europeans who wanted to make themselves known to me. Bush-telegraph had obviously alerted the majority of the Amiza managers as to the presence of a friend of their managing director being 'at large' in eastern Zaire. They greeted me warmly, squeezed my hand with the vice-grip of an orang-utan, and presented me with their business cards, at the same time telling me that if they could possibly be of any help during my stay in Zaire, I had only to make contact with them.

On a second occasion, the driver stopped in order to purchase one of two rock hyraxes or dassies *(Procavia capensis)* that were being offered for sale at the side of the dirt-track by some teenaged Africans. In spite of their rodent-like appearance, with some features of a huge guinea-pig with thick fur, short legs, short and pointed snout and small ears, dassies form an order of their own and are more closely related to an elephant than to any other ungulates. Due to the destruction of some of their natural enemies such as leopard, wild dog, eagles and other large birds of prey, in some areas dassies have increased enormously and, as a consequence, are easily hunted and provide a valuable protein food for Africans living at subsistence level. The driver wrapped his purchase in some soiled yellow newspaper and placed the dassie next to my kit-bag in the boot. The diesel engine roared into life and the driver exclaimed that dassies were very good 'inyama' – very good indeed.

The Amiza offices had closed by the time we arrived at Lubumbashi, but the driver had received instructions to take me to one of the flats in the compound normally reserved for company directors and VIPs.

The following morning, I rose just after 6am, breakfasted on hard-boiled eggs and rather soft cream crackers, stuffed all my belongings back into the kit-bag and went in search of Amiza's main office. On going down the steps and out of the

A plinth of clayey ground covered with reeds, a sleeping bag under a mosquito net and waterproof cape provided the 'home away from home' at Mulenda

Zaire Map

73

The rodent-sized dassie have rhinoceros-like cheek teeth and small hoofs on their toes which makes them more related to the elephant than to any other ungulates

door into the compound, I was immediately confronted by one of the watchmen, who indicated that he would guide me to wherever I required to go. I repeated Amiza HQ a number of times, and he obligingly led me towards the other side of the compound. The air was already hot and breathless. A nearby stand of gum trees exuded the strong characteristic odour of eucalypt oil from their finger-like leaves. Some motley brown poultry were nestling into their morning dust baths, while others continued with their incessant pecking at the ground, then resting momentarily to engage with their low-level murmurings to each other.

A polite, but somewhat apprehensive African, by the name of Ngoie, spoke to me in French and I was able to understand that he considered it would be impossible for me to fly to Bukavu that week. As this had been the same story that I had received in Kolwezi, I requested to be taken to the Air Zaire offices. On the short journey to the offices, I removed a spare expedition cloth badge from one of my pockets and kept it in my hand. On arrival, I asked in a polite, but in the most authoritative way that I could muster, to see the area manager and that such a meeting with him was a matter of considerable urgency. My request was followed by much agitated whispering among the staff behind the counter who were obviously uncertain about disturbing their boss for a person without an official appointment.

Doubtful that my request would be granted, I unclenched my right hand showing the embroidered expedition badge with the freedom torch motif. The revelation had the desired effect and within a quarter of an hour I had had an audience with the manager and, an hour later, acquired a plane ticket at a viable price for the morning flight to Bukavu.

I was one of the first passengers to board the Boeing 737 and was shown to a window seat on the starboard side. The rest of the seats soon filled up to seemingly bursting point and the paraphernalia associated with such African travel appeared to block all access to emergency exits and even in some places, the aisle itself. In spite of such an overcrowded cabin, the plane lifted off from Lubumbashi only five minutes behind schedule, at 10.50am. At just after noon, we landed at Kalémie, which is situated approximately half way up the west coast of the long sausage-like form of Lake Tanganyika. A couple of badly camouflaged army armoured cars were parked near to the eastern edge of the airfield, close to which were pitched a collection of khaki tents, arranged in a disorderly fashion, and a number of dishevelled military personnel were to be seen, either lounging or standing about like a small flock of sheep without the presence of an apparent leader.

A period of just under two hours was spent at a baked Kalémie while the plane was being refuelled and reloaded. During this time, two of the smarter soldiers stood guard by the 737 nervously fidgeting with their lethal-looking machine-guns.

During the flight from Kalémie to Bukavu, the plane clung to the lake's western shoreline, casting as it sped a streamlined shadow resembling the passage of a pilot whale skimming just beneath the lake's surface. The view of the voluminous, muddy waters that make up this central basin of the Rift Valley was quite breath-taking. With 32,900sq km (12,700sq miles) of water, Lake Tanganyika represents the eighth principal lake in the world, and the international boundaries between Zaire and Tanzania, and in the lake's northern area between Zaire and Rwanda Burundi, divide the lake along its great length.

Bukavu was 32km (51 miles) from the airport and I took a taxi once we had landed. The road wound its way like a worm through some neat and lush-looking coffee estates, past assemblages of thatch-plumed, mud-built African dwellings, before finally it descended and levelled out to the southernmost shoreline of Lake Kivu. As we approached the attractive township, the taxi had to pick its way through a generous rash of market vendors, past the small port and into the main street, before drawing up in front of the Hotel Metropole.

I was given a spacious room with a remarkable vista overlooking the lake itself, although, in keeping with everything else man-made in these regions, it appeared to have witnessed better days. However, the view of the lake nestling snugly within the embrace of the surrounding mountains was as equally as dramatic as those alpine lakes bordered by peaks in the Austrian Tyrol.

At dinner that evening, I learnt from a Mr Lulu Mwana-Kitenge, who told me that he was the manager of the Anglo-American Tobacco Company in Bukavu, that the best way to travel up to gorilla country in the Virunga volcanoes was to go to Goma on the northernmost tip of Lake Kivu, and that a vedette departed at 7.30 each morning. As the Virunga volcanoes had been one of my goals, I decided to catch the ferry and to travel northwards the following day.

By the time I had climbed on board the vedette at 7.30am, there was standing room only. The vedette took just over six hours to navigate its way through the mirror-like waters of Lake Kivu, to its northernmost port of Goma. During this time, it chugged past and between numerous islands, the majority of which, sadly, had been shaved of their blankets of forest.

On Lake Kivu, the international boundary between Zaire and Rwanda Burundi slews to the eastern coastline and does not slice the lake vertically in two, as is the case with Lake Tanganyika. It was while taking some photographs of the attractive Rwanda landfall to the east, that I was tapped on the shoulder by an ill-tempered looking African and, from his agitated gesticulation, conveyed that taking photographs of the boundary was strictly forbidden and an offence. I noted that he wore in his lapel a badge depicting Mobutu's red-flamed freedom torch. From his officious attitude, he could have been a minor state security official who probably considered that he had by a chance of luck stumbled upon a European agent gathering intelligence in this sensitive border area. The less I understood what he was saying, the more aggressive he became. Just when he started to pull at my camera case, either to take charge of my camera or to open the back of it to expose the negatives, I showed him my *Expedition du Fleuve Zaire* badge. Immediately, aggression turned to friendliness. The official addressed me as comrade, squeezed my hand and patted me forcefully on the back.

Prior to arriving at Goma, the traveller is afforded a dramatic view of the most westerly of the Virunga volcanoes which straddle the international borders of Zaire, Rwanda and Uganda. There are eight volcanoes in the group, the two younger ones of which, Nyirangongo and Nyamulagira, are still active. I had been told that the Nyirangongo's lava lake was a moonscape spectacle well worth seeing, but as gorillas were not to be found on the slopes of the two volcanoes, I realised that my short time in the region would prevent me from taking in such tourist attractions. The kernel of the Virungas is formed by three mountains: Mikeno, Karisimbi and Visoke. The area is divided politically by the Rwanda–Zaire border which extends from the summit of Visoke to that of Karisimbi. The eastern group of volcanoes, Sabinio, Gahinga and Muhavura, lies along the boundary between Rwanda and Uganda. The borders of both countries meet that of Zaire at the summit of Mount Sabinio. The Virunga Park in Zaire (formerly the Albert National Park) was my planned destination.

On arrival at the small port of Goma, just before 2pm, the security man appeared to conjure up a taxi from out of nowhere, then bade me farewell. The taxi driver did not bother to steer around any of the numerous pot-holes in the road, which caused the vehicle to bounce and shudder from one obstacle to another. He kept his hand on the horn throughout his reckless drive, miraculously missing other modes of transport and pedestrians, which were left, hidden in clouds of dust, in our wake.

The Hotel de Grand Lacs looks, as so many other dwellings in these regions, a mere apology of its former splendour, but I decided to make it my base. Conveniently, near at hand was Goma's Amiza headquarters, but when I arrived at its freshly whitewashed office, I was informed that the manager was away from Goma for at least a further seven days. I then tried the tourist office, but this was obviously shut with its heavy, green shutters firmly closed over the windows.

Back at the hotel, an Indian, who spoke English well, informed me that it was at

present impossible to get into gorilla country without first crossing the border to Rwanda. In order to check this information, I walked to the police station, where a surly, suspicious-looking sergeant meticulously studied my passport visa, my Kolwezi travel papers and at one stage held the latter up to the light as if he was looking for some inadequacy or forgery. Eventually, he informed me that if I were to travel over the border into Rwanda, I would not be granted permission to re-enter Zaire, for my passport visa clearly recorded that I could only enter Zaire at Kinshasha. It was evident that the Zairois officials had well emulated their previous Belgian masters, and I reluctantly came to the conclusion that I could not risk any escapade that might jeopardise my eventual return to the Zaire River Expedition.

So, my efforts to observe mountain gorillas in the Virunga volcanoes, which provided sanctuary to the major part of their numbers and distribution, had been thwarted. There was now no alternative but to return to Bukavu, and to attempt to see the eastern lowland gorillas that inhabit the Kahuzi-Biega National Park, which is situated on the south-western shore of Lake Kivu.

The implementation of protection laws, adequate policing of conservation areas, development of tourism and conservation education programmes, have greatly aided the gorilla's chance of survival (Sandy Harcourt)

The extremely gregarious
white pelicans usually
fish in tightly packed
flotillas, all submerging
their heads and necks at
the same moment

·6·

The Gorillas of Kahuzi-Biega

THE same evening as my voyage down from Goma, I met Charles Gracia, a Frenchman in his early thirties who worked in Kinshasa and had decided to take some leave in order to see gorillas in the Kahuzi-Biega National Park. On the previous Wednesday, he had already visited the park with Adrien Deschryver and although he had heard some vocalisations from one of Deschryver's habituated groups of gorillas, he had not had the good fortune to see any of them. Having already whetted his appetite in this way, Gracia was determined that he would not leave this part of the eastern lowland gorilla's distribution without having done everything possible to gain a glimpse of man's ancestral stock. So, in order to see how best we could arrange to achieve our mutual ambition, we decided to meet at 7.50 the following morning and get a taxi to take us to the Park Department's offices in Bukavu.

An African, wearing thick-lensed glasses, introduced himself at the offices as the park's accountant, and then proceeded to try to contact Deschryver on an antiquated wireless set. Having failed to make any contact at all, he informed us that he would take us to Deschryver's home, for only the Conservateur could give us the necessary permission to visit the gorillas.

On arrival at Deschryver's home, which was situated high up above the township and surrounded by a well-manicured lawn, studded spasmodically by impressive beds of the scarlet-flowered, purple-leafed, hybrid canas, we were informed that he would be away from Bukavu for a further few days, for the single-engined plane that he regularly flew had developed some mechanical problems which required attention in Kenya.

Three Belgians – two men and one woman – were patiently waiting in reception in order to find out whether they could visit the park that day. However, once they learnt that Deschryver was out of town and was not available to accompany them out to Kahuzi-Biega, they decided against making such a trip. Evidently a European had been badly hurt by one of the gorillas only recently. The Belgians related how some Pygmy trackers had made contact with the gorillas, but they themselves had become ill-at-ease, which in turn made the gorillas nervous. This had the effect of making the animals apprehensive which could make them act irrationally.

In spite of our mutual insistence that it was of vital importance for us both to visit the park, it soon became evident that the accountant was becoming increasingly irritated by our tenacity. Only when I produced my official international *Expedition du Fleuve Zaire* documentation as a last resort did his attitude change. I added weight to the official paperwork by explaining that I was making a special study of primatology with particular regard to the gorilla family.

Since 1937, Mount Kahuzi had been a zoological and forest reserve which, although meriting the classification of a national park, was not granted this status until 1970. In 1964 and 1965, while it was still classified as a reserve, the area suffered from serious depredations: trees were cut down and land cleared for cultivation and, above all, a great deal of hunting took place, which was particularly deplorable as the eastern lowland gorilla was among the chief victims. In 1965, Adrien Deschryver had stated that the gorillas were being hunted systematically by the Pygmies with the aid of dogs, nets and spears. Old males tried to defend their families but were massacred by spears. Females that took to flight became entangled in nets, while the sub-adults and juveniles that climbed into the trees for safety became a fine target for poisoned arrows. It was not long before almost all the young gorillas of Kahuzi had been exterminated and the remaining adults had become both aggressive and dangerous.

It had been against this type of lamentable back-drop that had stimulated Deschryver to attempt to preserve the remnant wild population on the south-west shores of Lake Kivu, and as ex-poachers frequently made the best game-keepers, he set about converting the Pygmies from poachers into guides. When the national park had been in existence for about two years, some of the gorillas that Deschryver had patiently habituated, began to realise that not all humans represented their enemies and visitors to the park were provided with the opportunity to see gorillas without too much danger. Even more rewarding, before long, nature had made amends and the number of gorillas increased.

The southern entrance to the park is only some 53km (33 miles) away from Bukavu and can be reached by a respectable tarmac road, that wound its way past several groups of human habitations that smudged the otherwise green tapestry of vegetation which beame more dense as we neared the park. The ubiquitous goats and chickens pulled and pecked at everything within reach and, under the shade of small banana groves, villagers could be seen pounding dried manioc into flour. Now and again, the road passed impressive-looking entrances to long drives, some of which snaked through well-planted coffee estates up to the mansion-like dwellings of the pioneers who had carved their profitable estates out of this most fertile of soils. Such vestiges of the Belgian colonial era were nostalgic reminders of both the good wrought, and sometimes the evil administered, by some of the earlier European settlers, especially in Zaire's formative days as the Congo Free State, when it was the private sporting reserve of the King of the Belgians.

On arrival at the barrier that stretched across the road and signifies the entrance to the precincts of Kahuzi-Biega, the accountant was greeted by two jovial-looking Pygmies and half-a-dozen or more apprehensive-looking soldiers. After considerable discourse, which appeared to become more and more excited, the two Pygmies and three of the soldiers climbed aboard our vehicle and we travelled a further 6km (10 miles) into the park. At 10.45am, we were dropped off and were told by the accountant that he would return to this same location just before sunset, and would rendezvous with our party then.

I quickly changed into some expedition issue US marine canvas and rubber-

Dug-out pirogues
represent the major type
of river and lake
transportation in eastern
Zaire (Richard Le
Boutillier)

soled jungle boots and Charles Gracia and I struck off into the montane rain forest preceded by the two Pygmy guides and subjectly followed by the trio of soldiers.

At first, we followed a well-worn trail into the denser foliage. Some of the bamboo's mature stems measured up to 8–10cm (3in) in diameter and their lush grass-like branches reached as much as 18m (59ft) into the light mountain air. In some places, it was possible to walk upright, in others in a more crouched position, whereas in some of the more impenetrable parts, progress could be made only by crawling on all fours.

Suddenly, our guides stopped in their tracks to examine some food remnants, faecal deposits and gorilla tracks that looked comparatively recent. Having picked up such a recent trail, they were as alert as tracker dogs and rarely spoke. They deftly cut their way through the thick blanket of bamboo with their metal pangas, gently laying it on one side and searching for every tell-tale sign of gorillas. After some forty-five minutes, there was increasing evidence that a group of gorillas had only recently traversed this particular trail: small piles of the sheafs of bamboo shoots, deposits of light-coloured faeces, broken branches and footprints in the sponge-like ground. Bamboo shoots are in season in this part of equatorial Africa between the months of September and February, so gorillas take advantage of this seasonal crop and gather handfuls of shoots, before settling down in a favourite spot to enjoy the delicacy of the hearts of the shoots. Once devoured, instead of discarding the shoots like an undisciplined baboon, the gorillas had left them in mounds of between four and twelve shoots per pile, arranging them in a surprisingly orderly fashion.

81

As we progressed further, my nostrils picked up the familiar effluvium musky odour of the gorilla. The guides listened carefully, then started to hack at some of the sturdier, ringed stems of the nearby bamboo to create as much noise as possible among the vegetation. Within thirty seconds, the noise of the pangas was responded to by a deep-bellied full roar from an adult male gorilla that must have been within 9m (30ft) of our small party. Another deep-bellied roar was followed by the breaking and crushing of bamboo stems. Approximately 6m (20ft) away among the heavy foliage, an adult male eastern lowland gorilla with an impressive jet-black head was sitting on the far side of a fallen tree. He gave a deep yawn, throwing his head back as he did so, displaying a fine array of ivory-white teeth, set within pinkish gums. He then shifted his position a little and suddenly stood up, executed the familiar gorilla chest-beat 'pok-a-pok-a-pok; pok-a-pok; pok-a-pok', and then disappeared out of view into the small valley beneath us.

George Schaller had made the first comprehensive field study of what was then described as a mountain gorilla in the late 1950s, and he highlighted the sensation that he had experienced on witnessing his first gorilla in the wild as 'the feeling of elation having finally reached a destination that has occupied the mind for months'. Similarly, Alan Moorehead in his classic *No Room in the Ark* wrote that when he first saw a big male in the Virunga volcanoes his one desire at that moment had been to go forward to the gorilla, to meet him and to get to know him. Now, having got to know something about the pressures that had recently been on the Kahuzi-Biega gorillas, I also wanted to congratulate any gorillas that I came across on their success in managing to survive at all.

Our small party followed in the direction of the gorilla's departure, negotiating some of the gorilla tunnels through the thick vegetation as best as possible. In one place, we disturbed a colony of small stinging ants, which covered our feet and legs like locusts, biting us with the effectiveness of a patch of stinging nettles. At approximately 2pm, while we were down in a swampy area, we heard another full-bellied roar of a male. The animal was obviously near but, because of the density of the vegetation, we could not see him. During the next forty minutes, the guides cut down some of the bamboos to try to gain a vista looking up the glade in the direction of the gorilla's vocalisations. It soon became obvious that the gorilla was becoming disturbed by our presence and on two occasions, he drummed his chest in an attempt to intimidate us, the first time with four 'pok a-poks' and on the second occasion with eight. There was another deep-bellied roar, which came from slightly further up the slope, then he did a characteristic bluff charge and bent over a large bamboo, but he never revealed himself. It would have been foolhardy to encroach on him further, so we did a flanking movement, and during the one-and-a-half-hour journey back to our transport, we came across gorilla feeding sites, the tell-tale sheafs of bamboo shoots and deposits of faeces. At one place, the guide found caught up in the vegetation a tuft of gorilla hairs. We also heard some gorilla noises which came from either a sub-adult or even a juvenile specimen, but we did not catch sight of the animal.

Charles Gracia and I followed our Pygmy trackers with sublime confidence, for neither of us had the remotest idea where the road was in relation to our whereabouts. The three soldiers stumbled about to our rear, seemingly oblivious to everything around them, other than having the basic instinct to follow the person moving in front of them. Just when the daylight was finding it more and

more difficult to find its way under the forest canopy and down through the foliage to the peaty substratum of the ground, the guides delivered us to the 'white man's route' through this mountain Eden, with a similar navigational skill and punctuality as if they were swallows returning to their nesting sites of the previous year.

The lifeless span of tarmac road ahead appeared incongruous compared with the lush tropical trappings of the surrounding montane rain forest. The accountant's vehicle had been parked under the shadows of an impressive stand of bamboo and when its side-lights were switched on to welcome us, the spell of having been seduced by the aspirations of mother nature was soon broken. As we sped back to the south-east to return our now jovial guides to their picturesque thatched and mud-built dwellings, and the three sullen Askaris to their unhomely-looking corrugated iron huts, I realised that I had, during the course of the day, experienced one of the highlights and most memorable occasions of my life.

It was not until the afternoon of Sunday 13 October, that I received word that Adrien Deschryver would be at his office in the Park Department's headquarters in Bukavu on the following morning.

On Monday morning, therefore, I met Adrien Deschryver, an athletic-looking, clean shaven man in his early forties, at his office. Having introduced himself, he turned and introduced his female assistant, Lee Lyon. Lee, in fact, had first met Deschryver while she had been a part of Anglia Television's production team which, some two years previously, had filmed the Kahuzi-Biega gorillas, resulting in a fifty-minute programme for their *Survival* series entitled 'Gorilla'. This

Gorillas glean from the dense stands of bamboo the seasonal crop of shoots and calmly feast on the delicacy of the hearts

There can be few more spectacular sights than observing gorillas in the wild and the incomparable opportunity of seeing them must not be lost

programme depicted the remarkable relationship between Deschryver and the groups of gorillas that he had become friendly with, especially his association with the leader of the main group, a magnificent silver-backed male called Casimir. So taken had Lee been by the life of this dedicated Belgian conservationist, that she had managed to gain a contract from Collins, the publishers, to write a biography of Deschryver. The company's managing director, Sir William Collins, was due to visit them the following month to quench his insatiable quest for knowledge about the animal kingdom – in this case gorillas – and to keep up his practice of paying field visits to his wildlife authors in the various parts of the world.

While Lee and I talked, Deschryver occasionally looked up from the papers that littered his desk and seemed to glance at me with a degree of reserved curiosity; I sensed that he was not totally at ease in my company. It was only later in the week that I was told why his initial impressions had appeared to be so reserved. As a child, he had first seen a large silver-backed male gorilla sitting by itself in a heavily barred cage in a European zoo. The cage had been dark, badly ventilated, with nothing in its embellishments to stimulate the gorilla's mind. To the young Deschryver, it had conjured up what life in a medieval dungeon must have been like for humans and, because of his abhorrence at the incarceration of such a majestic animal, he had disliked zoos and had not paid one a visit ever since.

I obviously shared his sentiments with regard to animals being kept in such a fashion. Perhaps, had I not been involved in helping the evolution of modern zoo science and the development of the zoo world to contribute something really worthwhile for the animal kingdom, I, too, may have maintained similar reservations about anybody hailing from a zoo background who wanted to feast their eyes on gorillas in the optimum of settings.

His attitude began to change towards me when I produced a copy of the Jersey Trust's tenth annual scientific publication, which embraced a number of papers on the Trust's specific conservation breeding programmes. As the Trust's first two gorilla births had occurred in the previous year, it detailed papers on the maintenance, breeding and hand-rearing of lowland gorilla, written by three members of the Trust's staff, including myself; there was a comparison of baby gorillas with human infants at birth and during the post-natal period, by the Trust's consultant paediatrician, and a preliminary report on the psychological development of two infant gorillas, written by two post-graduates from the Department of Psychology, University College, London. All represented a valuable insight into the type of important observations that can be made with the study of such animal species in captivity.

Only comparatively recently had Deschryver attempted to hand-rear a young gorilla that he had confiscated from some Africans who lived just over the northern border of the park. Regrettably, the hand-rearing failed but he now wondered whether, if he had applied the feeding regime that had been adopted by Jersey and had the variety of human baby-food preparations and additives been available to him, there would have been a chance to have kept his orphaned gorilla alive. Over copious cups of locally grown Kivu tea, all three of us delved into as many aspects of our knowledge of gorilla life as possible. It was soon evident from the exchange of information on our respective experiences, derived from the study of gorillas both in the wild and with those in captivity, that we all shared a great deal in common.

During the morning's session, I had been grateful to Lee for her obvious recognition of my enthusiasm for the welfare of the animal kingdom and in particular my fascination for gorillas. Such an awareness on her part had undoubtedly influenced Deschryver to regard me in a different light. Prior to leaving the offices so that they could attend to a pile of correspondence, Deschryver asked me in his quiet, unruffled way whether I would care to accompany them both as their guest to the park at 8.30 on the Wednesday morning. I almost hugged them both, took my leave and walked elated back to my hotel.

On our journey out to Kahuzi-Biega, I was keen to ask Deschryver as many questions as possible: what did he consider the estimated population of gorillas to be in the park; how many groups were now familiar to him; what was the chief threat to the gorilla population; what erosions to the habitat were being inflicted by human encroachment, etc? Fortunately for Deschryver, it was a speedy journey out to the park, with few delays on the well-maintained tarmac road. Lee was waiting for us at the park's entrance and greeted us warmly. She possessed that rare ability to make a complete stranger like myself feel welcomed and that she was pleased for me to have this opportunity to share their experiences with the gorillas.

The Pygmy trackers and two soldiers were standing to attention just inside the park gates to geet the Conservateur. The army personnel looked much smarter than on my previous visit and obviously regarded Deschryver as their 'Bwana mkubwa'. After a brief inspection of the soldiers, Deschryver turned his attention to the trackers and talked to them in their local tongue to bring himself up-to-date with the whereabouts of his two habituated groups of gorillas. While he talked, it was easy to sense the bond that existed between the trackers and their boss.

The Pygmies and the military men clambered into the back of the jeep and Lee sat between Deschryver and myself in the cab. A further ten minutes of motoring to the west brought us to a small clearing on the north side of the road, not far from the place where I had gained entrance into the mountain rain forest on my previous journey to the park. I quickly changed into my canvas US marine jungle boots, hung the usual naturalist's paraphernalia around my neck, then followed the trackers, Deschryver and Lee into the forest with, as before, the soldiers taking up the rear. On this occasion, they appeared to have much more confidence and no doubt the presence of Deschryver with his .375 rifle provided them with the security they so desperately required.

The trackers soon picked up the trail where gorillas had recently been foraging and they went about their duties with the stealth and quiet agility of felines stalking their prey. The trek had started just before 10am and before long we left the beaten track to follow the previous night's meanderings of the gorilla group that the trackers were diligently pursuing. Soon the tell-tale signs of gorillas appeared: carcases of bamboo shoots, so much the favourite of gorillas at this particular time of the year, lay neatly arranged on the ground and the familiar musky odour of the gorilla species hung in the air. The cool tranquillity of the montane rain forest was suddenly broken by the roaring and chest beating of an adult male gorilla. Deschryver considered that this male had come into the area from a different group to try to solicit some females away from the group led by Casimir, the elderly silver-backed male that Deschryver had become friendly with during the past six years. Deschryver felt that, with a male arriving from a different family, a certain amount of danger was apparent, for Casimir's family was obviously unsettled by the chest beating and roaring of the newcomer.

With the gorillas in such close proximity, Deschryver had taken over the lead position of our group and the Pygmies looked slightly more at ease in joining the two soldiers to take up the rear-guard. At 11.30am, a young male approximately six to seven years old came out of the vegetation to approach his friend, Deschryver, but when more chest beating from the alien male was heard, he withdrew to the security of his family group, which remained out of sight but evidently near at hand. This latter specimen, which had a slightly deformed arm, will mutually groom with Deschryver – illustrating the tremendous bond that can develop between man and beast, provided that the encounters are based on mutual respect and understanding.

Further down in the swampy area of a small valley, the male intruder was producing deep-bellied roars, beating his chest and making mock charges of intimidation but, because of the thickness of the vegetation, he did not break cover. During this time, Deschryver stood facing the direction of the noise, saying quietly 'Com, com, com, com' and mimicking the gorilla noise of pleasure. Our party rested between 1 and 2pm to coincide with the gorillas' midday siesta, which Deschryver believed should not be disturbed. Half an hour later, the gorillas began to move again and Deschryver came to the conclusion that as the animals were so disturbed by the newcomer, we would stand little chance of seeing anything more, so we started to retrace our tracks. Suddenly, however, Deschryver heard the snapping of a twig about 27m (30yd) to the right of him and, within two minutes, we came upon the large bulk of Casimir who was lying down with his back towards us, with six other members of his family to the rear of him. A large male was lying on his back in a totally relaxed position, his attention

Shy and Gentle Vegetarians

Gorillas are currently found in two distinct regions of Africa, separated by about 600 miles of tropical forest in the Congo Basin. Due to forest clearance for agriculture and commercial logging and hunting for food, their numbers and distribution have been greatly reduced in recent years.

In Equatorial West Africa lowland gorillas live in the southern Cameroons, the south-west corner of the Central African Republic, western Congo-Brazzaville, Equatorial Guinea, Gabon and a small population in Angola to the north of the Zaire River and in Nigeria along the southern border with the Cameroons. It is estimated that well over half of the 35,000 – 45,000 western lowland gorilla population remaining occur in Gabon.

The eastern lowland gorilla occurs in eastern Zaire and in 1980 was estimated to number 3,000 – 5,000 individuals. The highly endangered mountain gorillas are confined to the Virunga Volcano region which straddles the international borders of Zaire, Rwanda and Uganda. Two thirds of the conservation area lies in Zaire in the Parc des Virungas, and about 30,000 acres are in Rwanda in the Parc National des Volcans, with the remaining area being within the Impenetrable Forest Reserve in Uganda.

Extensive conservation efforts during the past twenty years have reversed declines in the mountain gorilla population, which now numbers between 420 – 440 animals, of which 280 – 300 are to be located in the Virunga Volcano Region.

Gorillas live in fairly stable social groups and, in most of these, there is usually only one silverbacked male present at any one time. Although the sexes are born in almost equal numbers, fieldworkers have found that silverbacked and blackheaded males may leave groups and live for a time either as 'lone males' or in a small bachelor group. Leader silverbacked males may well inhibit other males from mating and young male gorillas may leave their natal groups as they attain maturity and establish their own home ranges. Females may in turn leave established groups to join the males which thereby provides the mechanism for the formation of new gorilla groups, and prevents inbreeding.

(Photo courtesy of The Digit Fund)

divided between casually regarding the knuckles of his right hand and looking good naturedly in our direction. Two gorillas were tussling together like friendly wrestlers and a younger pair were making a fuss of Casimir who was asleep, while the seventh member of the group contemplated us from a sitting position, seeking some type of introduction and reassurance.

Casimir was an old silver-backed male when Deschryver first saw him in 1966, so he was considered to be well over thirty years old. He was now too old to keep up with the rest of his group, so No 2 or No 3 males deputise for him, and at intervals of two to three days return to him. It is interesting to note that the transference of leadership that was witnessed in Casimir's group had at that time never been observed by Diana Fossey in her extensive field-work with the mountain gorilla in Rwanda.

After half an hour, Casimir slowly began to wake up, rolled onto his side to face us, propped himself up on his right elbow, then gathered himself up into a sitting position. Only then could one fully appreciate the creature's size and magnificence. Deschryver mimicked the gorilla's welcoming noise and two or three of the group returned the greeting. Deschryver also chewed some vegetation, which is recognised by the gorillas as an act devoid of hostility. After fifteen minutes of mutual admiration between Deschryver and Casimir, the gorilla ambled off down the slope through the giant bamboos, followed reverently by the other six gorillas.

During the next hour, we followed the gorilla family, keeping as close to them as possible without wishing to disturb their late afternoon foraging. Some of the smaller specimens climbed high up into the trees, feeding on the red berries of a species of stinkwood. Gorillas are known to feed on two hundred or so vegetable food plants in the almost sterile montane forests of Kahuzi-Biega. During this period, four other members of the group appeared. On one occasion, Deschryver was trying to film a sub-adult female and was within 3m (9ft) of her, when Hannibal, a deputy leader of the family, broke cover, roaring and beating his chest in a well-practised bluff charge, to warn Deschryver not to encroach further on one of his relatives. Hannibal came within 2m (6ft) of us, whereupon Deschryver, not giving an inch of ground, repeated softly 'Com, com', and Hannibal retreated respectfully. On past occasions, Casimir had come up to Deschryver, grabbed him by the shoulder and rocked him to and fro, which is evidently a friendly interaction. But it was Deschryver's experience that it was possible to get as close to the family group and remain with them for such a long period of time only once or twice a year.

Three-quarters of an hour before dusk, we left the gorillas to settle down for the night, whereupon the females and younger ones climbed into nesting sites in the trees, while the senior males remained at the foot of the trees to slumber and keep guard.

Deschryver estimated that at the time there were approximately 250 eastern lowland gorillas in the national park and, with between 300 and 350 mountain gorillas inhabiting the Virunga volcanoes, he considered that the overall population was under 600 individuals. Owing to the disappearance of suitable habitat, it was no longer possible for gorillas to traverse the intermediate terrain and as such, the Kahuzi-Biega population would now have to survive in isolation.

National parks embrace some of the most fertile lands that remain, so that neighbouring farmers, having bled their top-soils to a state of land erosion, now

Members of the expedition's scientific group at Mulenda displaying Zaire's 'freedom torch' flag in honour of the visit to camp of the Luba District's Regional Chief and entourage

cast their covetous eyes over the lush grazing pastures of the nearest park. In the case of Kahuzi-Biega, some 300,000 people inhabited the region in close proximity to it and the authorities realised that, without the continued financial benefit of tourism, the park could well be condemned. In local politics, the pressure to release land for agricultural purposes is often difficult to resist.

Deschryver had recently attempted to introduce an orphaned infant from another group into that of Casimir's family. Although such an introduction was planned to be a gradual process and it ultimately ended in the infant's death, it did provide an interesting insight into the potential of such an introduction, especially if, in the future, there was the need to augment isolated wild populations, or even to supplement such populations, with captive-bred individuals. When Deschryver showed Casimir the ten-month-old infant with the object of familiarising the orphan with both the forest environment and the vocalisations of the sub-adult and adult specimens, he was accosted by Casimir who tucked the infant under his arm and returned to his family, placing it at the feet of an adult female who immediately picked it up to take care of it. Regrettably, because of the infant's age and the fact that the female did not have any milk, the unweaned infant died after a few days.

Although I was provided with the opportunity to visit Kahuzi-Biega again and my encounters with the gorillas were very special on each occasion, owing to the increased unsettled nature of the main habituated group, the sightings were much fewer and far between. Perhaps one of the chief stimulations of any type of field-

work is never actually knowing whether or not you are going to see what you are seeking; but, to the enthusiastic naturalist, having the opportunity to examine large spiders' webs, festooned between branches of lush vegetation and bejewelled with drops of moisture from the saturated air, to witness the countless multi-coloured and iridescent populations of insects, either crawling along or navigating their way through the dense canopy of vines entwining a small copse – all provide a type of magic and wonder of their own.

·7·
Life on the Lualaba

DAWN was just breaking over Lake Kivu as the road to the airport started to wind its way into the hills. A few cigar-shaped, dug-out pirogues caressed the reed-clad shoreline and the hair-line silhouettes of the ebony-skinned fishermen on the lake's calm surface were just visible. The first rays of the sun were starting to illuminate the sombre trappings of the forested slopes of Mount Kahuzi, the peak of which seemed to nod its farewell benevolently as the road tossed itself into a steep valley. The occupants of the thatched mud-huts were already fully occupied with their daily chores, the handsome womenfolk walking, like statues, with old oil cans filled with water balanced miraculously upon their heads, goats nibbling at everything within reach and the ubiquitous poultry pecking incessantly at the ground, with some of their number narrowly missing the wheels of the battered taxi as it sped, without any apparent care, through their midst.

It was a hot but uneventful flight south to Lubumbashi. The soldiers garrisoned at the airport at Kalemie did not appear to be awake when the plane landed just after 8am. By cab to the Amiza offices in Avenue Kasai, I immediately bumped into my previous helper there, Mr Ngoie who greeted me like a long-lost friend and took me to see the office's assistant director, Mr Kotchouey. As had happened during most of my meetings in Zaire, the initial outlook appeared to be bleak, with no available accommodation or prospect of transportation to Kolwezi. But, as before, the presentation of the 'To Whom It May Concern' letter signed by Amiza's Belgian managing director in Brussels, Jacques Feyerick, and my *Expedition du Fleuve Zaire* credentials, quickly transformed an almost impossible situation into one of great co-operation. One of the best VIP rooms, an invitation to dinner and a guaranteed vehicle to take me to Kolwezi the following day were all offered to me in an instant.

After lunch, I was pleased to have some spare time, for I had wanted to visit the Jardin Zoologique de Lubumbashi, which had been partly designed by the late director of the Royal Zoological Society of Antwerp, Walter van den Bergh.

During my tour of the zoo, it was apparent that, prior to independence, a considerable amount of money had been spent on its development and a great deal of thought had gone into its planning. There were a number of spacious moated areas for chimpanzee, gibbon, wallaby, to mention only a few; but in some areas, owing to the lack of funds for any type of redevelopment or even proper maintenance, the caging was unfortunate. However, the most favourable aspect of the zoo was that all the animals appeared to be in good condition and that the senior staff were proud of their wards and keen to do as much as possible for them.

It was regrettable, however, that the zoo exhibited so many species from other continents, instead of concentrating on their own national wildlife heritage. Ten years earlier, at a symposium entitled 'Zoos and Conservation' at the Zoological Society of London, the Duke of Edinburgh had suggested the possibility of establishing international zoos in countries which could not afford to establish their own zoos, not least in those countries which have large numbers of wild animals but where the bulk of the population have little or no opportunity of seeing animals in the wild. This would be one way of helping them to realise the importance and urgency of conservation. The duke's ideas seemed particularly pertinent with regard to the Lubumbashi zoo.

The following day, the Amiza truck left Lubumbashi an hour behind schedule, but we arrived at the Kolwezi Amiza office just after lunch. Paul du Nyn appeared to be as surprised to see me back in one piece as Mr Ngoie had been in Lubumbashi. After assuring him that I was intact and that gorillas were harmless animals with only one enemy, man, he arranged for me to be taken around to where the scientists had been originally billeted at the Victor Forest's flats. On arrival, the place was deserted, so I asked the driver to take me to where the expedition's HQ had been, which fortunately was still bustling with life.

Almost the first person I bumped into was John B.-S., who hailed across a forecourt, 'Ah, Dr Livingtone, you've returned.' I told John that it had always been my intention to return and then related to him and Ashley Barker some of the experiences that I had been privileged to have encountered with the gorillas of Kahuzi-Biega. John was obviously very interested and asked me to give an account of my experiences to one of the expedition's public relation co-ordinators later on in the afternoon as a press release was about to be issued.

Tony Macadam was a historian and writer on African affairs by profession, and had just completed his PhD studies at Edinburgh University. The interview, which was also recorded, was given to the expedition's *Daily Telegraph* correspondent, Hugh Davies, as well as being sent to the Voice of America for transmission. It was only later, while I was on my way out of Zaire at Kinshasa, that to my chagrin and dismay I saw examples of the type of poetic licence that had evolved from my interview and that had been published in various syndicated newspapers. Such captions as 'Gorillas Play Host to Zaire Explorer' and 'Mr Mallinson Out-bluffs a Gorilla', sensationalised what could only be described as a totally normal interaction between a habituated group of gorillas and their observers. It was a pity that this type of prostitution of the facts that usually confine themselves to the columns of gossip writers, should have occurred and embraced the quiet dignity of the gorilla kingdom. Hopefully, other syndicated reports presented my experiences in a more sympathetic and respectful fashion. However, one report concluded with the words: 'such an experience was the most exciting of his life for Mr Mallinson who has spent fifteen years studying the ape family throughout the world.' I am still wondering to this day, which apes in other parts of the world the reporter was referring to!

It was very fortunate that I had returned to Kolwezi when I did for, on the following day, the main part of the expedition was scheduled to move to Bukama, which represents the highest part of the upper regions of the Lualaba where the Colorado giant inflatables were to be launched. The group of scientists that I had been briefly billeted with before had had a successful field encampment beside a copper mine, while the tactical headquarters with the logistical support groups had been assembling the inflatables and stores in readiness for the river journey itself.

The enthusiasm of Dr Stephen Sutton, an entomologist from Leeds University, regarding the density of insect life that he had found in close proximity to the disused mine shafts was overwhelming. It was obvious that he considered that his exposure to such a diversity of insect life, in such a unique type of environment, was far more dramatic and significant than any of my encounters with the gorillas in Kivu Province. Andrew Patterson, a young botanist who was making a collection for the Royal Botanical Gardens, Kew, and Dorothy Bovey, a genial botanical artist whose driving ambition was to draw every plant in Zaire, could both well have been cast for a documentary film about the great Victorian collectors. The enthusiasm of this small, but select group of scientists was contagious, and we were all anxious to reach the Lualaba and see what such regions held in store.

At 6.30pm the following day, the main body of the expedition left the surprisingly well-manicured Kolwezi railway station, the building of which appeared to be an exact replica of any such small station which can be seen in both provincial France and Belgium. As TAC HQ had organised a plane to fly the expedition members to Zaire, it had now hired a complete train to convey us all, including the Zaire army liaison officers, to the bridge-head at Bukama.

The train journey throughout the night was somewhat erratic as the train stopped on the single-line track in the most unexpected places. When the engine belched its way happily into Bukama at 9.30am, it appeared that everyone from the entire region had turned out to witness our arrival. Perhaps, to the younger generation, from our various appearances, we resembled a gathering of international variety artistes; others, who recalled the four years of bitter fighting in this region between Tsombe's secessionist forces, the Baluba tribesmen and the European mercenaries, must have been reminded of those troubled days between 1960 and 1963, less than fourteen years earlier.

While the expedition stores and our personal kit were unloaded from the train, the Zairois liaison officers had difficulty in keeping the assembled crowds away from our possessions. Ashley Barker assembled the eleven-strong scientific party and requested politely that we should follow him to our intended billet, which was situated to the west of the township, on the banks of the Lualaba.

As our party wended its way along the main dirt road away from the station, we passed a number of burnt out and cannibalised remnants of war: old jeeps and a scout armoured car littered the storm ditches; numerous shops and houses were pock-marked to various degrees by shells. There appeared to have been no attempt either to repair or rebuild anything since the place had been repeatedly attacked and the European population had decided to desert Bukama for good. Even the Western-style post office, once the hub of all communication with the outside world, was still partially demolished as a result of a direct hit from an exploding shell some thirteen years earlier. Evidently, at the time of our visit to Bukama, one Belgian and one Greek were the only Europeans now living in the township.

Our billet was a long-vacated Western-type bungalow, with a large cement-floor verandah and a number of rooms carpeted with grey dust. The thin-gauge wire-netting of the verandah now resembled a sieve more than a protective screen

The centre piece of the Kahuzi-Biega National Park is the summit of Mount Kahuzi which rises 10,000ft above sea level to the west of Lake Kivu

against mosquitoes. Larger perforations were the obvious hallmarks of machine-gun fire, for similar scars were apparent in the decaying mortar of the outer wall of the bungalow as well as in the outer wall of the verandah. Although there were electric light fittings, Bukama no longer had any public electricity; a small African beer hall that boasted a generator was the only place to display such wonders of the twentieth century. The water situation was slightly better, for the supply was switched on for a few hours in the evening, but in no circumstances should the water be drunk.

For the third consecutive meal we dined on sardines. The supply had evidently derived from some British Ministry of Defence stores which, since the early 1950s, had already accompanied one expedition to the Arctic and two to Antarctica, as part of the emergency ration stores. Large slices of locally grown water-melon helped both to dilute and cleanse the oily make-up of our staple diet. Four crates of Simba beer seemed to arrive from nowhere, as a gift from the breweries. We therefore set about to do full justice to it and toasted our good fortune that TAC HQ had decided that our small party of entomologists, botanists, zoologists and

fish experts should make up an advance party to go ahead of the main fleet into the swamplands of the Kamolondo depression, downstream to the north. Ashley Barker informed us that we would be woken at 5am and that we must be ready to move out with our personal kit within the hour.

By 6 o'clock the following morning, we had dutifully scraped our mess tins clean of food, gathered up our respective kits and, donning jungle hats, ambled somewhat gleefully away from the rather depressing environment, which had witnessed so much more joyous days. On our arrival on the east bank of the Lualaba, the view of the river was an anticlimax. The shoreline on both sides was devoid of any real vegetation and a number of sunken freight barges and the wreck of a river steamer did nothing to enhance the barren scene with which we were confronted.

After passing under the road and railway bridge, we arrived at the place where three of the Avon S400s were ready to take our small party the 80km (50 miles) or so downstream. A British army major, a seasoned veteran of the Darien Gap expedition in Central America, welcomed us to his close recce group of inflatables, told us how we must don life-jackets, the technique of climbing into the Avons without capsizing them and how to store our kit. At all times, we were to obey the orders of the craft's skipper, for failing to do so might result in our joining the hungry crocodiles in the Lualaba. As the majority of the assembled scientists were well-seasoned travellers in their own right, we were apt to shrug off such potential hazards with a degree of badly concealed humour, which was not always appreciated by the regular servicemen who seemed to consider that the scientific part of the expedition were an unruly collection of people who should be reminded constantly of the folly of not strictly adhering to the orders of the day.

The party was asked to split into three groups and I selected the group led by the only civilian to be in charge of one of the recce group's Avon Specials, a delightful, soft-spoken architect from Newcastle, Bob Powell. Also sharing the inflatable was a Dr Alan Bartram, a rather bewildered-looking fish expert; Dr Peter Shrewry, a botanist from the Rothamsted Experimental Station in the UK; and a young entomologist colleague of Stephen Sutton's, Peter Hudson.

By the time the outboard-motors roared into life, a large crowd of Africans, predominantly children, assembled on the bank above us, all waving their cheerful goodbyes. It turned out to be a restful day for, since we had taken up the rearguard station, probably because we were all civilians, we did not even have to keep a watchful eye for the whereabouts of hippopotami, but rather we were able to relax and talk about our various ambitions and what we considered the Upemba swamps held in store for us.

As the river coiled its way sluggishly northwards, flanked on either side by beds of reeds and beyond by a rather featureless terrain before it was arrested by a horizon of bluish-grey hills, we passed a number of villages, with their mango groves, occasional palm trees and gatherings of smiling, waving children to whom we made it our duty to respond enthusiastically. This small flotilla of Avon Professionals and their para-military-like crews may have appeared to the onlookers as an unusual sight, but none of them could have even dreamt what spectacle was to be in store for them eight to ten days in the future, for the story of the giant Colorado inflatables, carrying the main expedition party, would doubtless be passed down from one generation to another.

Just before it was time to stop for lunch, the army captain in the leading Avon Professional signalled that there was danger on the port bow. Following the direction of his gesticulations, we could see, just to the lee of a sand-bank, the cavernous nostrils, large bulbous eyes and the delicate, twitching ears of a small family group of hippopotami. Their midday slumberings, in the coolness of the Lualaba, had obviously been rudely infringed upon by the whining of the outboard motors. In order to avoid the expected danger, most of the creatures instinctively submerged, whereas a half-grown specimen slightly panicked by emerging and running up onto the sand-bank, then realising that it was on its own, speedily returned to the safety of the water. Although the rest of the group had completely disappeared from view, it was their tactic to emerge suddenly, without warning, in the most unexpected of places. Fortunately, our leader had sufficient knowledge of animal behaviour to retire, as quickly and as peacefully as possible, from the scene.

We arrived at our destination of Mulenda in the late afternoon but, before we could establish our camp on the opposite shore to the large native village of

Mulenda on the eastern bank, permission for us to do so had to be obtained from the tribal headman. The Zairois army captain therefore visited the village and informed the chief that it was an honour to have the vanguard of such an international expedition choosing to encamp in his territory, especially as the expedition was under the patronship of none other than President Mobuto himself.

The necessary permission granted, we reached the western bank just before darkness settled over the shoreline. The kindly Ashley Barker delegated the SAS sergeant-major, Eddie McGee, to take charge of our eleven-strong group of scientists, while the forward recce group, the two liaison officers and Ashley Barker separated themselves from us, in order to set up their own camp. Eddie McGee attempted to remind our party about what had been taught three months earlier at the Royal Military Academy at Sandhurst. While some of the group struggled to hang their hammocks within a grove of banana trees, the members of the recce group were already sitting around a large camp fire, enjoying their intake of Simba beer.

The evening was both enjoyable and convivial, for the scientists and members of the recce group were in sufficient small numbers to exchange stories of past experiences in different parts of the world and to integrate well. Although the recce group had to return upstream to rejoin the main expedition at Bukama at first light the following morning, it was easy to sense the degree of greater understanding that had developed between the diverse disciplines that were represented around the camp fire. Such good communication would undoubtedly prove to be invaluable for the ultimate success of the expedition and the overall comradeship of the gathering seemed beyond doubt.

As the generous quota of warm beer started to relax those assembled around the camp-fire, apart from McGee who was a teetotaller, angry storm clouds could be seen gathering as they threateningly began to block out the pallid complexion of the full moon. It was obvious that we would be fortunate to escape the onslaught of a tropical thunderstorm before the night was out, and indeed, the waterfall that cascaded from the heavens quickly eroded the sanctuary of our hastily constructed hammocks and we took shelter under some fig trees.

The week at Eddie McGee's camp, although uneventful as far as my zoological studies were concerned, provided me with insight into the professional motivation of my scientific colleagues, the highly disciplined qualities of the SAS sergeant-major and of the leisurely life-style of the occupants of Mulenda. By coincidence, the two young explorers that had won their places on the expedition and who had been allocated to the camp to help McGee cope with the scientists, were both nineteen-year-old Jerseymen: Richard Le Boutillier, a very fit-looking farmer's son, who appeared to volunteer in a good-natured way for everything; and Peter Picot, a police cadet, who, like any good serviceman, preferred to reflect on the nature of the work before he became actively involved.

The quietly spoken Professor Harold Woolhouse, of Leeds University, was the senior botanist on the expedition, as well as being the senior academic among the eleven-strong complement of scientists in McGee's camp. Before making the first collecting trip to Lake Mulenda, it had been decided that some of the group should pay a courtesy call on the local headman. The recce group had left behind one of the Avon Professionals, which we used to ferry ourselves across the

Lualaba to Mulenda. Keith Thompson, a colleague of Harold Woolhouse and an expert on the water hyacinth, Stephen Sutton, Peter Hudson, Dorothy Bovey, Andrew Patterson, Peter Shewry, Alan Bartram and myself, followed the lanky figure of the scholarly professor along the muddy track that led us between the mud-built dwellings of the citizens of Mulenda, to the brick-constructed abode of the headman.

The headman was sitting in the shade outside his dwelling as we approached. With the aid of his carved staff of office, he rose with some difficulty to greet us. He appeared to have some type of tumour on his right leg and, although there was an estimated population of some four thousand in the area, there were no longer any medical services available, so both Harold Woolhouse and Alan Bartram were quick to inform him, in their scanty French, that within the next seven days there would be two doctors in the district, who could both look at his leg. We followed him indoors, sat on wooden stools around a trestle table and, as custom demanded, toasted his health in palm wine. Whenever we drank from the chipped pottery cups, one of the headman's younger wives would immediately replenish the contents and before long we realised that, what at first had seemed to be a mild beverage, was proving to be extremely alcoholic. Before the wine seriously affected our concentration, therefore, I considered that it was time to show the headman my field-guide to the larger mammals of Africa, by Jean Dorst and Pierre Dandelot, which contained well over two hundred colour illustrations. The headman was fascinated by the book's contents and when he came to the antelope section, his wizened face lit up and his blood-shot eyes rolled in expectation. Through Alan, he indicated that he would like to possess some of the larger illustrations to stick on the wall among a montage of faded magazine photographs. I replied that to tear even one page from such a book would instantly bring bad luck, and although I wished that I could leave the entire book with him, owing to my responsibilities to the expedition, which in turn was aimed at helping the people of Zaire, I was unable to do so. The headman appeared to be grateful that I had not yielded to his wishes and as a consequence brought bad luck to his household.

After we had taken our leave, with numerous handshakes and repeating *jambo* or *bonsoir* to everyone in sight, we erratically retraced our tracks to the Avon Professional that was to ferry us back to our camp on the western bank. Perhaps, in the history of the village of Mulenda, the occupants had never witnessed such a friendly group of Europeans passing through their midst. When, in fact, the expedition doctors did eventually arrive in Mulenda, they soon established that the indigenous population was rife with measles and that gastro-enteritis was rampant.

On our return to camp just before noon, it was obvious that Eddie McGee was finding it difficult to contain his military life-style and refrain from treating us like soldiers returning to camp somewhat the worse for wear, for undoubtedly, if we had been a part of a new intake of SAS recruits under his supervision, we would have been severely reprimanded. Instead, he had to satisfy himself by requesting us to help him get the camp into an orderly shape. Kit-bags had to be stored neatly by our hammocks, firewood had to be collected and stock-piled, water collected from the river and boiled in readiness for drinking; and reeds had to be gathered and then placed over the ground in the area adjacent to the fire, where we were to eat our meals and generally congregate as a group.

The collective effects arising from the protocol courtesy call of the morning, my attempts at trying to assist Eddie McGee to make the camp the pride of the Lualaba, a late luncheon of sardines washed down by a large can of Simba beer, resulted in the necessity of a siesta. No sooner had we settled into our hammocks, however, than we heard some unmelodious bugle sounds that were coming from the direction of the river. Startled by these unexpected sounds, we quickly rushed to the river bank and from downstream saw a galvanised motor-launch making its way towards our camp, the main occupant of the boat being the chief of the entire Luba area.

The Long-Tongued Okapi

The Okapi inhabits the eastern equatorial rain forests of Zaire. It was first described from some skin 'trophies' that had been collected in the Ituri forests in 1901 by Sir Harry H. Johnson. The animal was first classified as a kind of zebra, but upon close examination of the body and skeleton, was found to be the only living close relative of the giraffe.

These extremly wary and retiring animals are rarely observed in the wild, moving away into the shadows of the forest whenever disturbed. Their senses of hearing and smell are particularly keen, which assists them in avoiding danger. The overall body colour varies from maroon, deep red to almost black, and has prominent black and white stripes of varying width on the sides of their buttocks and limbs; such markings greatly assist their camouflage in the dense and damp forests they prefer.

The long tongues of the okapi are ideally adapted for their diet of leaves, fruit and seeds from many plants. Also, their tongues are sufficiently long that they are able to wash or clean their eyes with them. Although the Epulu Research Station, situated within the Ituri forests, was established by the Belgians to study the okapi, very little is known about its habits even today.

A few okapi have been maintained in captivity since 1918, with most of the animals being kept in European zoos. During the last twenty years their numbers have remained stable at between sixty and seventy individuals. In order to maximise the captive breeding potential for this species, the populations in zoos are now under co-operative management programmes in Europe and the United States. The first long-term scientific field study of the okapi in the wild is at present underway, being sponsored by the New York Zoological Society's Wildlife Conservation International, in co-operation with the Institut Zairois pour la Conservation de la Nature.

A helmsman nurtured the craft deftly between some old mooring stumps before it became comfortably embedded within the reed-bed of the shoreline. The chief's ADC, resplendent in an unrecognisable khaki uniform, peaked hat and a colourful sash, with his bugle hanging from a red lanyard from his belt, jumped from the bow of the boat, missing the bank by several feet, and sank to his knees in water. Humorous as the incident appeared, we all maintained the degree of serenity and respect that such an arrival demanded. After the ADC had pulled the launch to the bank, he scrambled up it and assisted the chief, followed by his most recent wife, to land. Whereas the chief was dressed in a light-weight tropical suit which would have looked more in place in one of the more sophisticated restaurants in Kinshasa, his teenage wife wore a traditional long, vivid green cotton *pagne*, which patriotically boasted two large prints of the president's head on both the front and back of the closely fitting garment.

The two Zairois liaison officers were quick to salute their peer, who informed us, through them, that he had been told about the whereabouts of the expedition by the river drums and by an official communication from the commissioner in Bukama. He had already let it be known to his tribe's people, who numbered some seventy-six thousand, that they should help the expedition as much as possible. The speech of welcome over, the ADC lifted the bugle to his lips and played two verses of the Zairois national anthem. As soon as the anthem was concluded, the chief donned a leopard-skin hat and took an intricately carved staff from the ADC, came up to our group and shook us all warmly by the hand. After a tour of inspection, the chief concluded his visit and McGee and the two liaison officers saluted and the rest of the encampment waved their farewells as the motor launch pulled away from the bank. The boat soon disappeared downstream, round a bend, towards Kalombo.

Our week on the western bank of the Lualaba, opposite Mulenda, passed extremely quickly. On a number of occasions, I accompanied my botanist and entomologist colleagues to Lake Mulenda, which could be reached only by travelling in the African dug-out canoe-type boats known as pirogues. First, we had to ferry ourselves in the Avon Professional over to the west bank and then walk for about half an hour before coming to the pirogues, where a guide met us. On each of these trips, we encountered a semi-tame white pelican which paddled up and down like a small fun paddle-craft at Disney World. It had been brought over from Lake Mulenda some two years previously and was constantly fed by the locals, and even when some of its cousin pelicans flew over to the Lualaba from the lake to join it, the bird never bothered to make the return journey with them.

The route to the lake took us through a cobweb of channels between the somewhat oppressive stands of papyrus that towered above us from their swamp-like terrain; without a guide, we could easily have become lost within such a labyrinth. Once we arrived in the more open waters of the papyrus-fringed lake, work commenced in earnest. Because of the shallow waters, we were able to wade up to our knees, gathering samples of water hyacinth, collecting insects that inhabited the papyrus, to aid the ecological studies, as well as collecting plant-life at random to help Andrew Patterson's personal collection.

On one of our trails from the pirogues back to the Avon Professional, we noticed several clay pots placed in crevices in trees. Apparently, the pots had been erected by children to encourage owls to inhabit them, for the villagers knew that

Giant inflatable raft.
37ft long made out of
heavy duty neoprene,
weighing approx 1 to 20
tons loaded. Accom-
modates up to 20
passengers and capable
of approx 8 knots in still
water (Richard Le
Boutillier)

whenever owls were in residence, there were far less rodents left to damage their crops. This enlightened and forward-thinking practice obviously had something to teach our party of accredited scholars from the Western world.

In a small mud-brick trading store in Mulenda, I examined various skins of animals that had been killed in the Mulenda area. The collection included an ancient leopard-skin, which was not for sale, skins of bush-buck, sitatunga, otter and a rather smelly skin of a spotted hyaena. I made friends with an olive baboon which was tethered around its waist to a tree outside the store. Species such as cane rats, crested rats, bush-pigs and crested porcupine were frequently on the menu of some of the more active inhabitants of Mulenda.

Apart from the friendly white pelican, a pair of spur-wing geese constantly patrolled an area just upstream from our camp and seemed totally to accept our presence. An African fish eagle habitually perched itself some 274m (300yd) away from us, high up in a dead tree which had a commanding view over the river's slow-moving waters; occasionally, it would toss back its white plumed head and utter its distinct cry, which is rightly acknowledged as the real voice of Africa. The delicate, long-legged African brown jacanas, or lily-trotters, were frequently seen expertly negotiating their way over the aquatic plant life in their endless search for insects. Also observed were a great blue touraco and a malachite kingfisher hovering over the river before it plunged into the water and snatched its quarry.

The day before the main river party joined us at Mulenda, six of us had gone across the river on Sunday to accept an invitation to attend a service in a smartly kept mud-brick church. The church was filled to capacity, but room was soon made for us between two rows of sparsely clad children. We settled down on the mud-constructed seats, which were covered with clean rush matting, and listened attentively to two Africans squatting to the left of the altar as they started to bang the wooden drums that were gripped firmly between their knees. The early morning sun directed its spiritual rays through an open cross in the wall above the mud-brick altar and as the drumming increased in momentum and the volume

Olive baboon (Roger Wheater)

had almost reached its crescendo, a feeling of expectation could be sensed; then, suddenly, the drumming ceased and the tall figure of the priest, appropriately attired in cassock and surplice, entered, immediately followed by five identically dressed women in multi-coloured cotton pagnes.

As the priest made his way slowly up the aisle, the female attendants started to yodel, the rhythm of their exaltations being immediately taken up by the congregation, who started to hum and clap their hands in unison, whereupon the drummers restarted their impressive African beat on their instruments. On reaching the altar, the priest turned to face the audience, held his hands above his head in a beseeching fashion and, in a rich and resonant voice, addressed the congregation in both his native Luba tongue as well as in French. Once the introductory address was over, the service erupted into chanting and harmonising, similar to that of Negro spiritual music from America's deep south. While the service progressed, the five attendants walked up and down the aisle, singing in their falsetto voices, imploring and stimulating the congregation to clap their hands and to chant even louder. One of the ladies possessed a small loud-hailer, to generate an even greater degree of emotion and enthusiasm from all those assembled.

The service culminated with choruses of 'Hallelujah' and yodelling. When we finally managed to extract ourselves from the almost suffocating atmosphere of the building, we all felt weak from the heat. As was now our accepted practice, we shook hands with everyone who wanted to, maintaining a friendly façade of smiles, before we eventually returned across the Lualaba to the refuge of our camp.

·8·
The Giant Inflatables

J UST before 3.30pm on Monday 28 October, we heard an excited crowd of Africans from across the river and, looking upstream, saw the main river party coming into view. *Le Vision*, the flagship of the river expedition, was at the head of the armada of inflatables and John B.-S. was standing up in the bows, wearing a mini solar topee, looking very much the part of a reincarnated Henry Morton Stanley.

Six Avon Professionals acted as outriders for the three giants which, apart from the flagship, had been named after their sponsors, David Gestetner and Barclays Bank. Although the craft had been designed in the USA to take tourists through white water on the Colorado river in order to see such spectacular sights as the Grand Canyon, here on such placid waters they resembled vast rubber mattresses.

During the daily 6pm radio check with Kolwezi, John beckoned me to the wireless for there was a message from Jersey announcing that Nandi had given birth to a daughter on the previous Wednesday. After 'skoff', John gave out the news of the day and presented the sailing orders for Tuesday, which included the decision for the flotilla to cast off at 6.30am and that we should be sailing through the following night to make up lost time and, hopefully, to take on fuel at Kalombo. He concluded by saying that Jeremy Mallinson had just received a message via the radio that a daughter had been born in Jersey, not to his wife (an over-long pause), but to his gorilla. I received a round of applause. Gerald Durrell subsequently christened the first female gorilla infant to be born in Jersey, Zaire, in recognition of the conservation objectives of the international expedition. On my return to Jersey, the *Daily Telegraph* published a photograph of Zaire in my arms, with a caption that the infant had been named Zaire in recognition of President Mobutu's wildlife conservation measures. On a later occasion, John B.-S. was photographed in Gerald Durrell's study, holding Zaire rather apprehensively.

I was allocated space on the *David Gestetner* and although the craft were designed to accommodate twenty people comfortably, apart from the great quantity of stores that were necessary at this early stage of the expedition, which included piles of firewood for fuel for cooking, the river party and the scientists numbered in excess of seventy people, so it was difficult to find a small space to deposit one's belongings and stretch out.

The captain of the *David Gestetner* was a gentle, retired Royal Marine captain, Mike Gambier, who was now training to become a school teacher. Among the twenty-seven passengers that the *David Gestetner* carried were Stephen Sutton; the three Peters (Hudson, Shewry and Picot); Lawrence Cook, a delightful entomologist who was a lecturer at Manchester University; and the two *Daily Telegraph* personnel, reporter Hugh Davies and photographer Ken Mason. The craft was made out of a heavy-duty grey neoprene material and was powered by a 40hp two-cylinder Mercury engine, which was expected to cope with having to propel up to 20 tons of load through the waters. Owing to the excess of weight that had been taken on board, it was fortunate that the expedition was following the flow of the Lualaba/Congo river, as opposed to attempting to push such a load upstream. In order to facilitate night travel, Land-Rover headlights had been fitted forward, which were supported by small Honda generators.

Whenever we approached any human habitation, that were peppered at irregular intervals along the reed-fringed banks, the villagers would wave and shout their greetings of *jambo, jambo*. On one occasion, when the inflatables pulled into the shore so that we could buy some water-melon for the evening meal, Peter Hudson purchased an immature fish eagle on which he had taken pity. The eagle had evidently been in captivity for just over a week and appeared to be remarkably tame. However, as soon as he brought it on board the boat, it elected to relieve itself of everything that it had managed to consume during the previous few days. The eagle was immediately christened Compo after the dehydrated expedition stores and as some of the now soiled kit had belonged to two crew members, Peter and his bird were ostracised to the stern so that whatever the eagle decided to do in the future, it would be lost down-wind.

We stopped just before 5pm and went towards the eastern bank of the river, well away from a native village, for although the African river-dwellers had all proved to be most friendly, our accepted standard of good manners and protocol resulted in too much time being wasted to make a regular habit of stopping in populated areas. We discovered that a grass fire had been recently active on the bank and, apart from collecting a good layer of charcoal over our boots and legs, we saw an interesting variety of dead and moribund snails whose very numbers pebbled the ground with their shells. It would have been a desolate area in which to have been stranded. For the night journey, in order to save fuel and to give the crews of the Avon Professionals some rest, all but one of their boats were put in tow, and they joined the ever-more cramped conditions of the giant inflatables.

A wind was getting up as we once more followed the slow current downstream. The tasselled heads of the papyrus started to sway, whereas the reed beds bowed their heads in unison to the prevailing winds from the west; as darkness fell, we all knew that another tropical storm was brewing. We rearranged our kit and protected ourselves as best we could, for although the canvas canopy over the middle of the boat had helped to protect some of the passengers from the intensity of the midday sun, it would have little effect in providing any real shelter from a tropical storm; besides, the centre of the boat was where the three-man crew were located, together with the wireless set and other important items of equipment.

Before long, the storm broke over us: the familiar period of stillness and humidity, then the start of the raindrops from the sky, the great crashes of thunder overhead, the streaks of lightning illuminating the heavens, followed by the storm clouds emptying their reservoirs of rain upon us. The downpour was so intense that the Land-Rover headlights could not pierce the cascades of water in front of them, and the captain slipped the engine into neutral.

Once the storm had exhausted itself over us and moved away to the east, the

The immature fish eagle
'Compo' soon learnt the
far-carrying almost gull-
like call that is one of the
most characteristic
sounds of the African
wild

moon broke through and illuminated the bedraggled flotilla. The flagship took up the vanguard, followed by *Barclays Bank* and ourselves. A young sapper NCO started to play 'Waltzing Matilda' on an accordion, and we joined in humming and singing. A bottle of Cape brandy was passed around, from which we took a sip. The Avon Professional recce craft located Kalombo just before midnight, but after making our craft secure to the old moorings on a jetty, we decided to remain on board and slumber through to sunrise as best we could.

In pre-independence days, Kalombo had been a prosperous trading post and Belgian engineers had constructed a causeway through the papyrus to a jetty which provided access to the navigable regions of the surrounding swamps and to the Lualaba itself. An old warehouse on the jetty stank of fish and seemed recently to have been more exclusively used to satisfy the local villagers' lavatorial needs, as opposed to the exhibition and trading of the wealth of fish life that could have been extracted, by a more energetic population, from the swamps.

The local chief arrived to greet us and presented John B.-S. with a hen and some eggs. John reciprocated with a bottle of whisky, then showed the chief around *Le Vision* and, through an interpreter, told him the aims of the *Expedition du Fleuve.*

As there was a great deal of work to be done on the inflatables in order to try to combat more effectively the heavy rain that was especially frequent at night and to keep both stores and passengers more dry, it was decided to unload most of the kit. We were requested to select our own sites in which to sling hammocks, for we were to remain at Kalombo for approximately eighteen to twenty hours. We had also to secure some more fuel, for evidently our reserves were now minimal. By

10am it was clear that the professional crews of the various boats would find our absence more profitable to their progress so most of the scientific support group slipped down the causeway and into Kalombo itself.

As Lawrence Cook was making a comparative collection of butterflies and other insects, and was keen to collect as much material as he could in this particular region, because very little collecting had been carried out in this area previously, I was pleased to accompany him and to learn something about the Microlepidoptera of equatorial Africa. Stephen Sutton and Peter Hudson made up the foursome and we set off through the village, with butterfly nets at the ready, in the direction of some large tree-clad kopjes in the distance.

From Kalombo, the giant inflatables descended some small chutes to the lower level of Lake Kisale. We passed islands of papyrus, conglomerates of floating weed and grasses, which were interlaced by the attractive water-lily. As we advanced northward to the middle of the lake, a small group of fishermen paddling their pirogues came to take a closer look at this most unexpected of sights. In places, their isolated houses, constructed totally from the reed beds, blended superbly with the surrounding scenery of lake and swamp. We anchored in the open waters of the lake while one of the recce boats went to seek the most suitable way between the papyrus to the Lualaba and so en route to Mulongo.

As we made our way northwards, we noticed a series of old navigational posts which were dotted about at irregular intervals. A number of the posts had rotted and subsequently had broken off at the water-line, now causing more of a hazard to boats than being beneficial; but since the aftermath of independence, no boats, apart from the occasional chieftain's launch and now our flotilla, had come this way. Apart from Lake Kasale's wealth of fish life, it also boasted a profusion of bird life. Cormorants, herons, pied kingfishers – all were taking advantage of the old navigational markers to perch above the lake's calm surface and to scan its shallows for their prey, whereas the moorhens and jacanas took full advantage of the carpets of floating vegetation to seek their meal of insects. Peter Hudson's fish eagle surveyed the scene with a degree of disdain, for all he had to do was to gape his beak at Peter, and a tasty morsel would be produced for him to peck and swallow.

A mist was hanging over the swamps to the east of us, and the pounding of African drums could be heard in the distance as we pushed off from the bank to commence another journey through the night. As darkness fell with the usual tropical suddenness, we left behind the haze and the mosquitoes as our boats steered a course in midstream down the well-ventilated Lualaba under a full moon in a cloudless sky that illuminated the reed-fringed shoreline.

We arrived at Mulongo at 8.30am where we were to meet Professor Geoffrey Haslewood, from Guy's Hospital Medical School, a world expert on fish bile, and Dr Keith Bannister, a fish expert from the British Museum (Natural History), who had just returned from ten days of collecting fish in Lake Upemba. As we were to spend twenty-four hours at Mulongo and the vicinity of the warehouse was as unpalatable as the one at Kalombo, while the military-orientated busied themselves with formal duties, several of the scientists slipped away carrying butterfly nets, plant pressers, bottles of insect spray, sketch pads, cameras, binoculars and a bible.

After an hour of so of walking through Mulongo and its environs, carrying out our respective collections as we progressed, a truck stopped in which John B.-S.,

Female gorilla born at Jersey 26 Oct. 1974 which was subsequently named 'Zaire' by Gerald Durrell in recognition of the expedition's conservation objectives (Phillip Coffey)

106

Black kites frequent savannah and open country near to lakes and rivers where they feast on carrion, small rodents or insect swarms

Ashley Barker and a major wearing a paratrooper's beret were travelling. I could see from our leader's expression that he was not pleased with our behaviour which was obviously amusing the local population. Some three years later, when I read the extract of this encounter in Richard Snailham's excellent book *A Giant Among Rivers*, I became fully aware of the reason for his stern reception. Snailham relates:

> At Mulongo we established the practice that all groups going ashore from the boats must be accompanied by a Zairois Liaison Officer. Its first application had odd results: when John B.-S. was driving to the mission for lunch he passed two parties of scientists unchaperoned. He stopped and told them not to move until a Z.L.O. arrived. The nearest place for them to wait was an open-air bar, to which they quite readily went. Unfortunately there was a shortage of Z.L.O.s that afternoon and the two parties had to stay there for a punishing six hours, knocking back bottle after bottle of expensive Simba on their empty stomachs. Little clear-headed scientific advance was made that evening.

It was, in fact, an extremely interesting session, for we had been joined by Mulongo's chief of police and some of his colleagues, who bought more Simbas for us than we did for him; and although our conversation may have been devoid of scientific substance, we discovered more about local life and customs in those six hours than perhaps any more orthodox investigator would have been able to glean over a number of weeks. On our way back to the river in the late afternoon, John's personal assistant, Pamela Baker, showed me an immature thick-tailed bush-baby with which she had just been presented. I resisted stroking the animal in case it sank its needle-like teeth into me, but gave her some advice as to how best to feed and look after it. On our arrival at the warehouse, I was introduced to two pet kites belonging to Roger Sweeting, another fish expert. Both birds had very full crops, but finding themselves encircled by an admiring group of scientists, they immediately regurgitated their respective meals.

By the time we left Mulongo at 7.30 the following morning, the *David Gestetner* had also taken on a board a couple of chameleon which Compo gazed at with great enthusiasm. Whether a bird of prey would eat a chameleon is unknown, although perhaps their astonishing ability to camouflage themselves has never provided an eagle with the opportunity to sample chameleon meat.

In places the river banks became quite high and it was evident that the Lualaba was gathering more momentum having extracted itself from the swamps and lakes of the Kamolondo depression, and although the water was still low for this time of the year, it was flowing northward in a more determined way. We arrived at Ankoro some twenty-two hours later, having travelled through the cool of the night without the constant nuisance of mosquitoes.

It had been planned to remain at Ankoro for a forty-eight hour period and in the absence of any suitable camping site near to the confluence of the Luvua with the Lualaba, we took up residence in another run-down warehouse which was adjacent to an equally dilapidated jetty, which seemed to be constantly surrounded by school children. Ashley Barker arranged a meeting of all the scientists on the river party in order to establish how best we could take advantage of the time. I decided to remain with the entomologists and to continue my exploration of the bouquets of butterflies that were to be found in these regions and to learn about them from Lawrence Cook.

Ankoro was an extremely run-down and impoverished town, yet less than fifteen years ago it was a prosperous centre of trading. Passing through the town

Mission de Sacré Coeur

with its boarded-up shops, unkempt gardens and pot-holed roads, we came across a 75–100 bed hospital that had been completed in 1960, when it was handed over to the new regime. A smart, elderly hospital orderly proudly showed our small party some of the wards and spacious verandahs, but explained that there was no longer any electricity, running water or doctors; and apart from the occupants of a laundry room, next to an impressive operating theatre, the place was deserted. The orderly explained that he acted as a midwife to the constant flow of women who considered that even the laundry room was a safer place to have their babies than in the town's garbage-filled slum dwellings. The completion of the hospital must have seemed a dream come true to those who had been responsible for its construction; now, in spite of the zealousness of its sole orderly, it would not be long before the single-storey modern buildings fell into a state of decay and tropical growth would reclaim the site for itself.

A little further along the road to the south, was an imposing relic of post-colonial decline – a neo-romanesque church, built in the style of a cathedral, which had been the headquarters of the Mission de Sacré Coeur and which had been completed in 1934. Shortly, a late-middle-aged Roman Catholic priest arrived and opened up the building to show us something of its former glory. The red-brick twin towers stood defiantly above the iron-studded hardwood western door, and as its great hinges creaked when it was pushed open, clusters of bats fell from the darkness of the high-vaulted ceiling before they returned once more to their tightly packed roosts. Stale air and dust enveloped the nave and chancel, and the carved wooden stalls were splattered with bat droppings, whereas the industrious armies of white ants had streaked the paving stones of the aisles with their excavations.

The African priest asked us to follow him up the steep spiral staircase that led to the bell tower, so that he could show us the view from the commanding position over the surrounding countryside. To the east, we could see the well-defined course of the Lualaba and observe how the swamp-like terrain to the south had now receded to a more thickly vegetated landscape. We learned that the bell had been cast in 1827 in Caen and had been presented by a citizen of that attractive city in Normandy, France.

When we thanked the priest for his hospitality and joined him in a short prayer of personal thanksgiving, one could only feel a degree of despair for those missionaries who had been responsible for the construction, exactly forty years earlier, of this centre of Christian teaching, for such an achievement must have resembled a miracle. It was only to be hoped that those who had dedicated their entire life's striving for such a goal, would not have to return to witness how seemingly futile were their endeavours, nor the building's ultimate fate of ruination.

When we returned to our encampment around the warehouse in the late afternoon, I showed a group of school children the colour illustrations of my Dorst and Dandelot field-guide to the larger mammals of Africa. This generation of Zairois had obviously never previously seen such a printed book and were fascinated by its contents, especially as they were able readily to recognise some of the species that occurred in the region.

The following morning, I was awakened by the same group of children with a tribe of conspecifics in their wake, who all appeared to be carrying wicker baskets

The civet has well developed scent glands in the perineal region, secreting an oily substance used for territorial marking. This product is used in perfume manufacture (Phillip Coffey)

of various shapes and sizes. The first to be examined contained a remarkably agitated young crested porcupine, which was sitting at the bottom of the basket, quivering his quills and stamping with disgust at being constrained in such a fashion. Next, were a couple of African civet cubs, which were between six and seven weeks old and which spat their protests at being man-handled. This particular common species of Viverridae had been one of the first species of which we had made a study at Jersey, so I photographed the cubs, as well as measuring and weighing them for comparative purposes.

The contents of a basket was emptied out in front of me, to reveal several perplexed chameleons whose periscope-like eyes revolved in robot fashion, quite independently of each other. Then a smaller basket, with a snake neatly coiled in the bottom of it, was produced. As I was unable to identify the species and had no idea whether it was venomous or not, I decided to leave it well alone. A pied kingfisher, with one of its legs attached to a piece of string, was held in a young boy's hand. Through the liaison officer, I told them that they would be very good if they released, in a safe place, all the animals that they had brought to show me, and that I would be very saddened, and perhaps would have to tell President Mobuto, if I learnt that any of the animals presented had not been liberated. In a gesture of goodwill, the boy handed me the kingfisher, whereupon I untied the string and launched the bird into the air.

The last live animal to be shown was a four- to five-month-old olive baboon, tied around its waist with a length of shabby rope. It confidently strutted its way up to me, as if it already knew about my particular fascination with the primate kingdom. I requested the children to sit down and, to their great amusement, proceeded to show the baboon the colour illustrations of the eight different *Papio* species that are to be found in Africa. The baboon appeared to be particularly intrigued by the bright colorations of the West African mandrill and delighted the children when it flattened its ears at me and made a grab to tear the page from the book.

Finally, I was shown two crudely cured skins of adult civets and it was not difficult to conclude that they had been the parents of the two, now desolate, cubs. As I had now achieved the full attention of the children, with the help of a sympathetic translator, I strung together some Aesop-type fables, the message of which I hoped would guide those assembled and, in the future, would prevent them from capturing and killing animals unnecessarily.

On the final night at Ankoro, after the O-group meeting, when it fell to the scientists to present an account, for the expedition's log, of our daily investigations, the Reverend Basil Pratt held a service on the banks of the Lualaba. Hurricane lamps illuminated the improvised cross, which consisted of two crossed paddles lashed together, and while we were bitten relentlessly by mosquitoes, we listened to the padre's short address, recited prayers, and sang some hymns. At the end of the service, the heavens opened with the onset of another tropical storm and the congregation had to flee to the refuge of the crumbling warehouse.

We left Ankoro at midday and passed to the west of a long, slender island that boasted a fine stand of *Borrasus* palms as well as some healthy-looking agricultural workings. The temperature was high and the previous night's downpour had made the atmosphere extremely humid. The river banks were becoming monotonous and, apart from enjoyable conversations which were frequently among what we all now considered ourselves to be, the crew, it was a relief to stop for the evening meal at 4.45pm, which enabled us to be well on our way again prior to sunset.

The night's journey northwards proved disastrous. In the absence of any navigational lights on the river in the Kabala area, we nearly collided with a railway bridge. When the *David Gestetner* swerved to take evasive action, it almost deposited some of its crew, who had been slumbering on its pontoons, into the river's murky waters. After this, it was steered up a wrong channel and the giant inflatable became marooned on a sand-bank. In order to lighten the craft, a number of us had to disembark and then spend a considerable amount of time trying to manoeuvre it back so that the outboard engine could once more decide its course.

On another occasion, when a churn of tea was being transferred rather clumsily onto our bows, it toppled and fell into the river. In spite of the fact that the churn was quite buoyant, it took us some thirty minutes of going around and around in ever-diminishing circles in the water, before we succeeded in retrieving it. No medals for good navigation would have been handed out for that night's operations, and, as we had been informed that day that bandits, hostile to Mobutu's political party, were active in this region, it was a relief that none of them had elected to attack us during our somewhat erratic nocturnal meanderings.

We arrived, approximately 2km (1.2 miles) to the south of Kongolo, in the middle of the night, where we spent the rest of the dark hours attempting to sleep, while the giant inflatables relaxed like marooned killer whales on the river's muddy shoreline. At 5.30am, we were asked to take all of our personal kit off the *David Gestetner* to an old, former club-house which, although, like everything else in Kongolo, we found to be extremely run-down, it was the best accommodation we had encountered. This proved to be my last time on the Lualaba for, after the planned three-day stay at Kongolo, most of the scientists and support team were to travel on a specially hired train to Kindu, while the boat crews were to take the inflatables through the 16km (10 miles) of cauldron-like rough water and chutes, along what was referred to as the Gates of Hell.

It had been just north of Kongola that H.M. Stanley, having travelled through East Africa by Lakes Victoria and Tanganyika, had first seen the Lualaba on 17 October 1876. John B.-S. recalls in his book *In the Steps of Stanley*, his boat's arrival at Nyangwe on 13 November, and seeing the place where Stanley was reputed to have launched the *Lady Alice* on 5 November 1987, as well as being shown an avenue of mango trees that had been planted about 1886 by a Baron Danis, in commemoration of the event.

Only twelve years before our arrival in Kongolo the township had recorded one of the worst blood baths of the post-independence civil war. At a mission, we saw a plaque commemmorating the Martyrs of Kongolo, twenty-one priests who had been murdered at the mission, only one priest having survived. The massacre had occurred after the withdrawal of Tshombe's Katangese gendarmes from the area and drunken Congolese soldiers had run riot, beating the priests with bicycle chains, shooting them and then, in some cases, committing acts of cannibalism. It was difficult to comprehend that such atrocities had ever occurred in this now peaceful and tranquil setting and that it had happened so recently.

In spite of its size and rather startling appearance, the okapi, a close relative of the giraffe, remained undiscovered in its equatorial rain forest home of the Ituri forests, in Eastern Zaire, until 1901 (Marwell Preservation Trust)

Although I had had every intention of visiting Station de L'Epulu, close to the Ituri forests, to see such rarities as okapi and Congo peacock, because of the political and logistical problems, the transport from Kisangani east to Epulu could not be guaranteed. The okapi, the only living close relative to the giraffe, was made known to science by Sir Harry H. Johnston as recently as 1901. It was first to be classified as a zebra but, on close examination of skins and skeletal material, it was found to be a member of the giraffe family. These secretive animals are rarely observed in the wild and it is doubtful whether any European had seen one alive before 1907. Their chestnut-maroon, velvet-like coats are black and white on the limbs and over the rump. Their senses of hearing and smell which assist them in avoiding danger, are particularly keen.

A few okapis have been maintained in world zoos since 1918, with most of the animals being kept in Europe. During the last twenty years their numbers in zoos have remained stable at between sixty and seventy individuals, and it is gratifying to know that the captive populations in European and North American zoos are now under an international co-operative management programme. Two tame okapis are kept in the grounds of President Mobutu's palace at Kinshasa.

It had been the American ornithologist Dr James P. Chapin who first described the Congo peacock, which is the only true pheasant to be found in Africa. Dr Chapin's first clue that there might be such a bird in the Ituri forest came in 1913, when he collected a single secondary quill from a tribesman's hat. He next discovered similar feathers in two old mounted and incorrectly identified birds in a Belgian museum. He finally discovered the new species in 1937. Since then, live specimens have been carried to European and American zoos, with the Antwerp Zoo, Belgium, having contributed so much to the establishment of a viable captive population of this increasingly threatened species. The Jersey Trust has had individuals of the Congo peacock on breeding loan agreement from the Antwerp Zoo since 1972, and have recorded almost each year the successful breeding of this exceptionally oriental-looking peacock.

During our five-day stay in Kindu, the five of us who were leaving the expedition at this stage, were provided with the use of one of the Avon Professionals, so it was utilised to the utmost by carrying us into regions where we could undertake as many investigations as possible. During these studies we observed a small group of the Malbrouck vervet monkey, which represents the most widely distributed form of the thirteen recognised subspecies of vervets. Its coat was strikingly lighter than that of the other members of this species that I had previously studied, both at the Jersey Trust and in three other locations in Africa.

As we travelled north to Kisangani, a rump-spotted guenon was seen in the gallery forest some two hours upstream from Kindu and later it was found to be the most common of the guenon family – belonging to the Diademed guenon group. The baboon of the Western Rift Valley is represented in this region by one of the seven races of Anubis baboon and two different family groups were observed.

The Congo peacock was first discovered in 1937 and represents the only true pheasant to be found in Africa (Phillip Coffey)

Vervet monkeys have a wide distribution and are split into several well-defined groups due to its high degree of adaptability (Roger Wheater)

To the north-east of Zaire lies the Garamba National Park which was founded in 1938 and now represents the last refuge for the only viable population of the northern white rhinoceros. In the early 1960s the population of this northern race was estimated about 1,000 individuals, but by 1966, because of the presence of Simba revolutionary fighters, the population was reduced to approximately one hundred. Since 1984, when only twenty or so animals remained, the international conservation community (IUCN, UNESCO, WWF, Frankfurt Zoological Society) have effectively combined forces to manage intensely the remnant wild population of this genetically diverse species.

The resources that have already been expended for its conservation, and the interest and willingness of Zaire to conserve the species, fulfils the flagship nature of the northern white rhinoceros for conservation in this region of Africa. Although the captive population numbers only eleven individuals, a 1986 Rhinoceros Workshop strongly recommended the integration of conservation programmes for the wild and captive populations.

With fewer than fifteen founder animals known to exist for both the small wild and captive populations, it is recommended that every effort be exerted to expand the wild and captive populations as rapidly as possible from their small founder bases. In the autumn of 1987, it was significant to record that two calves were born in the Garamba National Park, and sightings of two or three individuals of this northern race had been observed for the first time in southern Sudan. Also, that through the efforts of the IUCN Species Survival Commission's Captive Breeding Specialist Group and the co-operation of the Dvur Kralove Zoo in Czechoslovakia, which owns nine out of the eleven captive population, every

116

effort is being made to transfer animals to facilitate the best possible breeding potential between stock held by Dvur Kralove, London, Khartoum and San Diego zoos.

The dramatic decline of the northern white rhinoceros has also been mirrored by the hapless African black, or prehensile-lipped, rhinoceros, which is at present being shot to extinction by poachers to supply a market principally financed by an oil-rich Arab kingdom, where its horn, an outgrowth of matted hair seldom weighing above 3.9kg (8½lb) sells for as much as $30,000 per kg (2.2lb). In North Yemen, the horns are made into ceremonial dagger handles, whereas in Asia, they are sold for medicinal purposes. It is prices like these that have caused such a catastrophic decline of an animal that was portrayed as a charismatic mega-vertebrate in the earliest European cave drawings, dating back 20,000 years and which has, as a species, inhabited the earth since the early Palaeocene period.

In the early 1800s, there may have been as many as a million black rhinoceroses in Africa, but because of uncontrolled hunting and the spread of human settlements, this number was reduced to around 100,000 by 1960. During the last twenty-seven years, the population has plunged dramatically to 60,000 in 1970, 15,000 in 1980, 8,000 in 1984, to less than half that amount today. With the rhinoceros now having been reduced to approximately 3,800 individuals, they cling to life in small pockets of habitat that have been set aside, at least on paper, for their protection; but even in these areas, they are subjected to the type of plunder that is increasingly causing scepticism as to the species' ultimate chance of survival.

By 1984, the black rhinoceros had been virtually wiped out in many African countries, although at that time the Zimbabwe rhinoceros population remained stable and may even have increased. The Kenyan rhinoceros population had

During the last twenty-five years the population of the northern white rhinoceros has crashed from about 1,000 to less than twenty animals (Roger Wheater)

declined from around 20,000 in 1970 to less than 500; and today the fragmented population is being relocated into heavily protected fenced areas, on both private land and in national parks. Since 1980, the Zambian population of some 3,000 rhinoceroses in the famous Luangwa Valley has been subjected to intensive poaching, which has brought its numbers down to about a hundred individuals. A similar-sized population in the Selous game park in southern Tanzania is said to have been reduced to a handful within eighteen months.

With an estimated 1,700 rhinoceroses still to be found in Zimbabwe, the majority concentrated in the Middle Zambezi Valley, Zimbabwe's Rhino Survival Campaign has done everything in its power to help fund capital items including boats, vehicles and a helicopter, to aid the anti-poaching and translocation operations. Since the inception of Zimbabwe's Department of National Parks and Wildlife Management anti-poacher patrol, some seventy-five poachers who have come over the border from Zambia have either been killed or captured, but during the same period a further 230–250 rhinoceroses have been destroyed.

As successive rhinoceros populations tottered on the brink of extinction, in early 1985 well-equipped bands of highly motivated poachers armed with AK-47 assault rifles or Chinese SKS semi-automatic guns finally reached the last remaining bastion of wild rhinoceroses in Africa: Zimbabwe's Middle Zambezi Valley. Only a few months earlier, the importance of this remaining wild and viable population of black rhinoceros had led UNESCO and IUCN (International Union for Conservation of Nature and Natural Resources) to accept part of the region as a World Heritage Site.

At the turn of the century the southern white rhinoceros was thought to have

Rhinos on the Brink

It will take more than love to save the rhinoceros. The hapless African black, or prehensile-lipped rhinoceros is at present being shot to extinction by poachers to supply a market principally financed by an oil-rich Arab kingdom where its horn, an outgrowth of matted hair seldom weighing more than 3.9 kg sells for as much as US $30,000 per kg. In North Yemen, the horns are made into ceremonial dagger handles, whereas in Asia, they are sold for medicinal purposes. It is prices like these that have caused such a catastrophic decline of an animal that was portrayed as a charismatic mega-vertebrate in the earliest European cave drawings, dating back 20,000 years and which has, as a species, inhabited the earth since the early Palaeocene period.

In the early 1800s, there may have been as many as a million black rhinos in Africa, but due to uncontrolled hunting and the spread of human settlements, these numbers were reduced to around 100,000 by 1960. During the last twenty-nine years the population has plunged dramatically to 60,000 in 1970, 15,000 in 1980, 8,000 in 1984, to less than half that number today. With the rhinos now having been reduced to approximately 3,800 individuals, they cling to life in small pockets of habitat set aside, at least on paper, for their protection; but even there they are subjected to the type of plunder that is increasingly causing scepticism as to the species' ultimate chance of survival.

At the turn of the century the

southern white rhino was thought to have become extinct, until only a few survivors were found in the Umfolozi area of Natal, South Africa. Strict protection and careful management have brought the southern race of this species back from the brink, with about 3,500 white rhinos now living in various countries of southern Africa and in world zoos.

The excellent results of such conservation measures provide some grounds for hope that national and international co-ordinated management strategies, encompassing both wild and captive populations, will prevent the further plunder of the five species of rhinoceros in Africa and Asia, and in particular halt the black rhino's drift into oblivion.

become extinct, until a few survivors were found in the Umfolozi area of Natal, South Africa. Strict protection and careful management have saved the southern race of this species from extinction, with about 3,500 white rhinoceros now living in various countries of southern Africa and in world zoos. The excellent results of such conservation measures provide some grounds for hope and national and international co-ordinated management strategies, encompassing both wild and captive populations, will prevent the further plunder of the five species of rhinoceros in Africa and Asia, and in particular prevent the northern white and the African black rhinoceros' extinction.

Kindu represented the finale of our participation on the Zaire River Expedition, and, prior to flying via Kinshasa on our return to Europe, we were entertained to a rehearsal by a troupe of some thirty Zairois maidens, assembled in lines, dancing and chanting. The pièce de résistance of the show was when an elderly man, in full tribal dress with head mask, danced an authentic tribal dance with a much younger Zairois in her long cotton pagne. This appeared to depict a cock and hen bird in a courtship ritual. As the dancing developed, the chanting of the singers grew louder and the rhythmic beating of the drums gathered momentum. The tall African, having worked himself up into a semi-frenzy, produced a long needle and suddenly plunged it into his mouth and out through his left cheek – but not a drop of blood was spilled. The chanting and drumming immediately stopped, with the hen bird fluttering around her needle-impaled male, as if the final act of conception had just taken place.

The hapless black African rhinoceros has been reduced from around 100,000 in 1960 to a population of about 3,800 individuals to-day (Phillip Coffey)

119

·9·

To North of the Brahmaputra

D URING the 1970s I became increasingly involved in national and international bodies dedicated to co-operative breeding programmes and
wildlife conservation in general. I therefore started to participate in an increasing
number of workshops and conferences, all of which provided a wealth of
information that helped me to gain a much greater awareness of the importance of
conserving biological diversity. Those working at the Trust also came to recognise
that conservation biology was inherently multi-disciplinary and so the Trust
adopted a multi-faceted approach with a much wider range of conservation
activities than its earlier pioneering work in the development of captive breeding
programmes for threatened species.

Participation at the First International Conference for the Conservation of
Fauna and Flora of Madagascar provided the opportunity to visit this great island
of red lateritic soil and to gain a privileged glimpse at some of Madagascar's
unique indigenous fauna and flora, nine-tenths of which occur nowhere else in the
world.

Some four-hour train journey to the east of Tananarive, the Reserve of Perinet is
chiefly remarkable as the best remaining example of eastern rain forest, as well as
for the spectacular number and variety of wild lemurs. The prima donnas of the
reserve are undoubtedly the largest of all lemurs, the indri, that have a stump of a
tail, long slender hind limbs and enormous hands and feet. These characteristics
are typical of vertical clingers and leapers, aiding them to move among the
preferred larger branches and vertical trunks. The long, soft, fluffy fur is strikingly
marked with black and creamy white patches which break up its outline in the
forest, making it difficult to see. Their faces are slender and foxlike and their ears
attractively fringed with long fur. There was no doubting their loud cry, which
could be described as mournful howling.

An early morning flight from Tananarive took us over faunal deserts to the
isolated township of Maroantsetra, on the great island's north-eastern coast. After
a short journey by truck over corrugated earthen roads, past water-gorged baobab
trees, we arrived at a small field laboratory. Nearby, a tree was embraced by a
wire-mesh cage that held captive an aye-aye – man's most odd-looking and
primitive cousin. About the size of a cat, it was completely black, with large
nocturnal eyes, bare bat-like ears and a tail like a splayed-out brush. Its middle
finger lacked the flesh of the other fingers and represented an elongated nail, an

adaptation to assist in its feeding habits when tackling food such as the interior of coconuts.

By launch we visited the forest-cloaked island of Nossi Mangabe, situated in the Bay of Antonoogil, 6km (4 miles) away from Maroantsetra. At the time of our visit, Nossi Mangabe had just been declared a special reserve and Dr Jean-Jacques Petter and Dr Peyrieras had caught and transferred from the mainland ten aye-aye and released them on the island. Although we were unable to see any of these most secretive and nocturnal of primates on Nossi Mangabe, on a trek I took with Jean-Jacques and his wife, Avril, up one of the precipitous hills to a small weather station, we saw a small family group of the white-fronted lemurs. Although no monitoring of the release of the aye-aye had taken place, recent field studies have revealed the tell-tale nests of the species, and successful reproduction has taken place.

The only other lemur species that I was able to see in the wild state was in a restricted area behind a camp of the French Foreign Legion, on the northern tip of Madagascar at Diego-Suarez (Antsiranana), where, twenty minutes before sunset, a group of five crowned lemur could be seen feeding in the trees taking little notice of us. This sub-species to the mongoose lemur is mostly confined to this region and had the military authorities to thank for its survival, for if the restrictions governing the area were to be lifted, it was considered that the vegetation would soon disappear, the lemurs deprived of their sanctuary and in all probability they would be taken for food. A trip to the forest reserve of Montagne D'Ambre included seeing the dramatic Grand Cascade where the moisture from westerly winds created clouds of mist. At the smaller reserve of Ankarana, which failed to reveal any further lemurs, provided the sight of some of Madagascar's

The Zoma or Friday market in Tananarive, the capital of Madagascar

121

exquisite bird life, including their malachite kingfishers and the type species of the drongo bird.

In March 1983 the Jersey Trust became a signatory to an agreement with the conservation authorities in Madagascar to promote close relations between the Trust and the Malagasy parties concerned, which undertook to co-ordinate activities for the benefit of endangered species. Since this time the Trust has funded technicians from Madagascar to undertake periods of training in Jersey, as well as some of the Trust's staff spending time at Parc Tsimbazaza helping to advise on the establishment of parallel breeding programmes. More recently, the Trust has been directly involved in the establishment of an on-site breeding programme for the world's rarest species of tortoise, the angonoka, or plowshare tortoise, as well as carrying out fieldwork on remnant wild populations.

The well-known lemur specialist and zoologist Alison Jolly recently wrote that, after some 165 million years of separation from eastern Africa, the world's fourth largest island faces an ecological crisis of the first magnitude. Whereas Madagascar's first wave of extinction eliminated a relative handful of species, today's extinctions are far more drastic, undercutting the survival of the Malagasy themselves. She concludes that, for their own sake, the Malagasy now must heed their own proverbial advice: 'Be like the chameleon – keep one eye on the past and one eye on the future.'

Two separate visits to India in connection with the rediscovery and future conservation measures for the critically endangered pigmy hog, from the 'thatchlands' of the Himalayan foothills of Assam, provided a fascinating insight into the complex problems that were facing conservationists within the sub-continent of India.

My arrival in India coincided with Calcutta coming almost to a standstill because of a one-day strike, or 'hartal', that had been called by a Maoist-inspired trade union. All the shops were closed and well shuttered against pilferers, public transport was at a standstill, and the streets were as deserted of the twelve million population as was practicably possible, while the creamy-coloured sacred cows walked about in nonchalant abandon.

The armed airline bus moved cautiously through the sprawling city, passing the blazing white marble stones of the Victoria Museum and the numerous deserted statue plinths where viceroys and state governors had once stood, and deposited passengers at their respective sanctuaries. My hosts in Calcutta, and throughout my forthcoming stay in Assam, were the old-established tea firm of Williamson Magor & Co Ltd, which had commenced business in 1868 and now had in their agency some thirty-four tea gardens, the majority of which straddled the thatchlands of the Himalayan foothills to the north of the Brahmaputra, in the north-eastern frontier state of Assam. It had been in this region of India that I was to be provided with a unique opportunity to examine and study two species of mammal, the pigmy hog and hispid hare, the former of which, according to some authorities, had been considered extinct for some twelve to fifteen years.

It had been Pearson St Regis Surita who had collected me in his company's chauffeur-driven car from the Indian airline's town terminal and had conveyed me to the elegant Williamson Magor dwelling in Penn Road. Pearson had been a well-known sportsman in his younger days and, after retiring from active

The largest of all lemurs the indri has a stump tail, long slender hind-limbs and enormous hands and feet, typical of vertical clingers and leapers (Quentin Bloxam)

participation, had become one of the most popular broadcasters on sport, in particular for his regular commentaries on the Indian cricket team for both the BBC and All India Radio networks. His professional career had involved him in public and press relations in Calcutta and, almost within an hour of meeting me, he had filed a biographical account of my involvement with wildlife for his column 'On the Scene' in the *Calcutta Statesman* that was to appear the following day.

Like so many present-day conservationists, Pearson had been for many years a keen 'shikari', both with rifle and shot-gun, before giving up the role of hunter in favour of being an observer of wildlife. Because of his interests and the nature of my investigations, Pearson had been given the job of escorting me to Assam, as well as being my travelling companion throughout the duration of my investigations in the land of tea gardens.

It had been the 'rediscovery' of the pigmy hog during March 1971, after an extensive fire had swept through some 80km (50 miles) of the tall-grass thatchlands in the Mangaldai sub-division of Darrang District, Assam, that had eliminated various reports that this miniature and unusual member of the pig family had been extinct for over a decade. It was the naturalist, B.H. Hodgson, who first wrote about the pigmy hog in 1847, when he described 'a new form of hog kind or Suidae' in his paper that appeared in the *Journal of the Asiatic Field Society,* Bengal. He had commented that it was incredible that so tiny an animal should have effectively resisted man until that time.

During the summer of 1969, while on home-leave in Jersey, a monocled, ex-Indian army tea planter, Captain Johnny Tessier-Yandell, had contacted Gerald Durrell to see whether the Trust would be interested in any of the animal species that inhabited the area in which he was now working. The Tessier-Yandells had previously presented the zoo with their pet Indian otter, Chips, and were anxious to help us in any way they could. Gerald Durrell asked Johnny Tessier-Yandell whether he had heard of any reports on the pigmy hog and Johnny, as he stated later, 'fired with the enthusiasm generated by discussions with Gerald Durrell', returned to Assam later that summer to put in hand the investigatory work that was necessary to track down this diminutive, little known, wild pig.

With the co-operation of his friends from the tea plantation, by interviewing a great number of the respective tea-garden labour force and other local inhabitants, and correlating all these various reports which narrowed the suggested sightings down to a confined area, Tessier-Yandell came to the conclusion that the pigmy hog population had not totally disappeared in the Mangaldai division of northern Assam, although in what numbers they remained, only further investigations would divulge. As the investigatory work continued throughout 1970, Gerald Durrell was kept up to date and informed of all possible sightings and developments, which became increasingly promising.

As a result of such encouraging reports, Gerald Durrell expressed interest in establishing at the Jersey Trust a captive breeding programme for this little-known species and, in collaboration with the Fauna Preservation Society, investigated the possibility of mounting an expedition, ostensibly to seek out the pigmy hog and hopefully to secure a viable breeding nuclei. The Survival Service Commission of the International Union for Conservation and Natural Resources (IUCN) was also contacted and agreed in principle that such an expedition should be mounted. However, the pigmy hog species was unable to wait for the proposed expedition to get under way and to come and detect them, for, as a result of the extensive fire within their sanctuary of tall-grass thatchlands between the Himalayan kingdom of Bhutan and Assam, a small population had fled south into the Williamson Magor tea garden of Attareekhat.

Such a dramatic reappearance was recorded by Tessier-Yandell who cabled Gerald Durrell from Bindukuri on 12 April 1971, stating 'splendid news, sounder of nine pygmy hogs in hand. Positive personal identification.' With such an acceleration of events, it was evident that a conservation strategy would have to be worked out quickly that would hopefully ensure that this species which had been considered to be extinct, would be secured for posterity.

By the end of April, some seventeen pigmy hogs had been rescued from the thatch fires, as well as having been saved from the pot: and as tea planters, not surprisingly, were not particularly well versed with the management of captive populations of such exotic species, Gerald Durrell requested me to go to Assam to provide comprehensive advice with regard to suitable accommodation, feeding, servicing and general maintenance of the animals, as well as to record as much as possible about this little-known species both in captivity and in the wild state. So it had been under the financial sponsorship of the Fauna Preservation Society's Oryx 100% Fund that I had flown out to India in order to investigate, advise on the conditions in which they should be maintained and to make recommendations for the future.

After a respectful introduction to the company's Managing Director, B.M. Khaitan, and the passing on of good wishes from one of his co-directors, Richard Magor, who had been responsible for making the decision to host me during my stay in India and whom I had seen during my transit through London, I settled down with Pearson to work out my itinerary and the logistics of our forthcoming tour of the pigmy hogs' last sanctuary to the north of the Brahmaputra. My passport was taken by a runner to secure the necessary visa and, with the temperature in the mid-nineties and a relative humidity of a similar extreme, Pearson and I were driven to a luncheon with Anne and Bob Wright. Anne was Calcutta's WWF (India) representative, as well as the Secretary of the Calcutta Wildlife Society and, as such, had contributed a great deal to wildlife conservation. We spoke at length about the reappearance of the pigmy hog and the type of conservation measures that should now be adopted to ensure its survival. Before taking our leave, I promised to keep her fully informed of my findings and to send her copies of reports and any photographs that I considered would be of use to her publications.

In the afternoon, I had arranged a visit to the nearby Alipore Zoo, prior to meeting up again at with Pearson for dinner at the Calcutta Cricket Club. A large lake constituted the centrepiece of the zoological garden, which was surrounded by entanglements of lush tropical vegetation, studded here and there by more orderly beds of purple-leaved, red-flowered canas, all of which appeared to be appreciatively bathing in both the high temperature and the humidity.

Colonies of night herons, pigmy cormorants and fruit bats shared the lake shore, islands and the large expanse of water with flamingos, pelicans, sarus cranes and waterfowl. Three to four months earlier, visitors could witness the famous sight of thousands of waterfowl, in particular the whistling teal and gargany duck, seeking sanctuary on the lake during the daytime, before moving off in great flocks to feed during the safety of the dawn and twilight hours, to the numerous waterways that interlace Calcutta's environs.

The tour of the reptile house with one of the zoo's many curators, coincided with feeding time, which represented a somewhat macabre spectacle. A Russel viper had just been presented with a handful of small song-birds to devour; the latter fluttered around the glass-fronted cage, not surprisingly, in a state of uncontrolled panic, while the viper bided his time until such food items stimulated him sufficiently to make his first strike. A reticulated python had just been presented with a large live brown hen; a cobra was surrounded by a collection of suspicious-looking frogs; while another cobra was in some difficulty in trying to rid itself of a small water snake, which, in an attempt to save itself, had managed to wrap itself tightly around the serpent's neck. All the reptiles represented in the house looked in fine condition, but it was only regrettable that the zoo authorities had found it necessary to feed live food, when in the vast

The conspicuous cobalt and bright ultramarine blues of the Malachite kingfisher's crest and upperparts contrast magnificently with the rufous colour of its cheeks and underparts (Quentin Bloxham)

majority of cases this is not considered to be at all necessary.

The prize of the zoological collection for me was a pair of the rare golden langur (*Presbytis geei*). The magnificent species of langur was only first fully described as recently as 1953 by the naturalist F. P. Gee, in the *Journal of the Bombay Natural History Society,* for he had first observed it east of the Sankosh river in Assam, close to the border with Bhutan. While in the shade, the golden langur's coat looks almost a uniform deep-cream colour, but on moving into the sun, it takes on the appearance of a bright golden mantle, while the black mask of the face resembles a dark shadow within a sea of richness.

A family of white tigers lazed in the mid-afternoon sun, their large forms remaining motionless while their blue eyes raced after almost everything that moved within their sight. A well-displayed chronological tabulation recorded the birth of the zoo's original pair at the Maharaja of Rewa's palace in Madhya Pradesh in 1953, which had been the source of all such white mutants.

The first breeding at the Alipore Zoo had occurred in 1960 and since that time, some eighteen cubs had been reared successfully to a third generation breeding. A pair of the rare Asiatic lion was also on exhibition, but these had totally succumbed to the day's temperature.

Although some of the Victorian-style buildings were in great need of replacement, the zoo's director, Mr Mandal, explained how anxious he was to modernise his zoo but that he was entirely reliant on the local municipal authorities for the development costs. Owing to the current dire economic situation of this region, it appeared unlikely that any improvements could be made to the status quo unless outside aid could be provided to help in the development of the zoological park and to make it an important educational resource.

Early next morning, I was back at Calcutta's airport. After a stringent security check, with soldiers standing about with automatic firearms, the passengers for the India Airlines' flight to Gauhati were almost herded across the tarmac to the awaiting Dakota, in which we sat for a good half hour, becoming warmer every minute, as we waited for the plane's engines to splutter into life. Due to the political tension that had recently manifested itself between India and East Pakistan (Bangladesh), Indian planes could no longer fly over Pakistan territory, so flights from Calcutta to Assam had to be routed to the north of West Bengal before they turned to the east through the corridor bordering the kingdoms of Nepal, Sikkim and Bhutan to the north, and East Pakistan, now Bangladesh, to the south.

Fortunately, although totally unwittingly, I had seated myself next to a window on the port side of the Dakota, so just after the plane had altered course to the north-east towards Darjeeling, I was afforded a breathtaking bird's-eye view of Nepal's rumpled foothills and, as the monsoon clouds rolled by, I could see beyond large formations of black rocks that were lightly streaked with snow, which rose in ribs to form an amphitheatre of peaks in the Everest chain. Pearson lent over to tell me that, provided the clouds continued to drift across the horizon, there would be a sporting chance to gain a glimpse of the snow-capped southern face of the world's highest mountain, which, only two days previously, had thwarted an attempt by an international mountaineering expedition to conquer its 8,850m (29,028ft) peak.

Mount Everest was named after the Surveyor-General of India (1830–4), Sir George Everest, and represents the only mountain in the entire range to bear the name of an individual. Approaching it from the lowlands of Nepal, it lies northernmost at the head of a glacier-filled valley surrounded by peaks swathed in snow, with some of the summits fluted by ice-furrows before somewhat dramatically descending in flying buttresses to the more humble Nepalese foothills beneath. Suddenly, the clouds broke, revealing the majesty of the snow dome of Everest's summit. Such a spectacular sunlit horizon was both remarkably dramatic and exhilarating, especially as, up to half an hour previously, I had not had the slightest idea that such an opportunity would have presented itself.

We landed at Gauhati at 10.30am and were met by Gordon and Yfke Simpson, who were to be our chief hosts in northern Assam. An impressive bridge spanned the muddy waters of the Brahmaputra as we travelled over to the north bank at the beginning of our 130km (80 miles) journey over comparatively well-graded dirt roads to the Borengajuli Tea Garden, which was close to the Bhutan border in the Mangaldai subdivision of Darrang District, the very heart of the newly acclaimed pigmy hog country.

Borengajuli was close to both Attareekhat and Paneery, the two tea gardens where the majority of the pigmy hogs, that had been saved from the thatch fires, were now being accommodated. Gordon was in overall charge of the three estates, and Borengajuli, of which he was superintendent, had the largest of the tea factories in the region. The spacious bungalow was surrounded by a coarse green carpet of closely cut grass. The generously sized verandah was open on three sides, with two large ceiling fans which revolved diligently in an attempt to generate a cooler movement of air, in a temperature which was already hovering around the mid-nineties. The surrounding garden boasted of numerous blossoming red flamboyants, as well as bright yellow laburnum trees which were stationed on the garden's perimeter; beyond these, could be clearly seen a fine stand of tea bushes, pruned to approximately the waist height of the tea pickers, all of whom were gently protected from the intense rays of the midday sun by the canopies of the delicate shade trees.

In spite of the early start from Calcutta, both Pearson and I were anxious to set eyes upon these newly found gems of the hog family as soon as possible; so we arranged with Gordon to visit the Attareekhat garden in the late afternoon, for we had been told that only recently one of the sows had given birth to four young. The opportunity to observe, weigh and measure such young was a heaven-sent chance to establish a series of comparative data and norms that had not previously been recorded for the species.

A converted chicken-house was home to the pig family. Our arrival at the run startled the three adults, one male and two females, that were accommodated together, for they emerged from a small stack of cut thatch to dash in fits and starts up and down the far fence-line of the run. In many respects, they resembled a dwarf version of the European wild boar. Their pelage was of a blackish-brown colour, suffused with rusty red, with the bristles at their longest and coarsest at the nape of the neck and behind the shoulders. Apart from its great reduction in size, pigmy hogs measure 25–60cm (20–24in) from the tip of their pointed snouts to the base of their short tails, and are only 25–30cm (10–12in) high. The only really significant contrasting characteristics are their forequarters, which appear proportionately less massive than their hindquarters, and their jaws, ears and tails are proportionately much reduced. As the trio realised that we were not going to encroach into their immediate territory, they soon calmed down and ambled around their pens, before the two females decided to retire to the comforts within their mound of thatch.

In the adjacent pen, but with a thoughtful grass screen between them which provided some important additional security, was the female with her four young. As it was possible to go in and handle the young without the mother experiencing undue trauma and stress, I asked the planter's permission to handle all the four young in order to sex, measure and weigh them, as well as to examine the mother, and measure and weigh her too. The young resembled toy pigs and some four to five yellow-brown stripes could be detected running along the back of their sleek, brown bodies. Such lack of distinct striped 'humbug' markings is in contrast to those possessed by the piglets of wild boar in Europe, northern Africa and Asia. The mother had no under-hair on any part of her body and her skin was of a grey-brown complexion. Furthermore she possessed only three pairs of teats, compared with the six pairs of other pigs.

When B.H. Hodgson had first described the pigmy hog less than 125 years previously, he had made reference to the fact that it appeared to have the disposition and resemblance of the peccary, he observed:

The herds are not large, consisting of five or six, to fifteen or twenty; the males fearlessly attack intruders, charging and cutting the naked legs of their human or other attackers with a speed that baffles the eyesight, and a spirit which their straight, sharp laniaries renders really perplexing if not dangerous.

At the time of our visit to Assam, there were some fourteen adult specimens, three male and eleven female, and four young, which were split up and maintained in three separate locations. Apart from the four adults and four young that were kept at Attareekhat, one male and three females were accommodated at the nearby Paneery tea estate which, although this came under the overall jurisdiction of Gordon Simpson, was managed by Robin Wrangham, and the pigmy hogs were lovingly cared for by his wife, Anthea. The remainder of the captive population, one male and two females, were being kept at the Budlapara tea estate, which did not come under the auspices of the Williamson Magor Agency. In order to promote conservation measures in this area of north-eastern India, the Assam Forestry Department, which was also responsible for the running of the Gauhati Zoo, the Williamson Magor Agency and a number of other animal conservation-minded planters had recently formed the Assam Valley Wildlife Scheme, of which India's then Prime Minister, Mrs Indira Gandhi, had just accepted the invitation to act as its patron. From the outset, it was decided that the Attareekhat and Paneery animals should be held under the trusteeship of the Assam Valley Wildlife Scheme.

During the next few weeks, I divided my time, accompanied on the majority of occasions by an ever-patient Pearson Surita, between observing the two captive populations of pigmy hog to which I had access, both during the daytime and at night, as well as to travelling into some of the tall grass thatch area bordering the north of the tea gardens adjacent to the Himalayan foothills, that represents the remaining habitat of the pigmy hog species. Over the last century, pigmy hogs have been recorded at intervals along the southern Himalayan foothill savannah belt which stretches from southern Nepal in the west, through Sikkim, north Bengal and parts of southern Bhutan to this region of north-western Assam. As William Oliver reported some nine years after the pigmy hogs' reappearance in 1971, the former and present distribution range for this species can be exclusively equated with the availability of the tall-grass savannah that typically occurs along the southern edge of the Himalayan foothills.

The thatchlands, sometimes also known as the 'terai', is a well-drained, essentially flat habitat but, regrettably, owing to the encroachment by immigrating settlers on the pigmy hogs' remaining habitat, the harvesting of grass for roof thatch and so much of the remaining area being subjected to dry-season burning, the species had been split up into small pockets of population that were becoming increasingly subjected to the pressures of direct competition with mankind. Apart from the deprivation of the hogs' cover and food, and its protected status, it was still being hunted for meat; and the more I travelled through some good samples of the remaining habitat, the more it was obvious that there was, on the whole, only paper conservation coverage in such remote corners, and that it was almost impossible for the authorities to implement some of the conservation measures that would provide hope for the species' real chance of survival.

On a number of occasions, we traversed the densely vegetated area along the border of Assam with Bhutan. At the time of my visit, the thatch had grown to the height of approximately 1.5–1.8m (5–6ft), but as the monsoon rains materialised, the tall grasses grow up to at least double that height, which, if they are not cut or burnt, provide an excellent sanctuary for the pigmy hog species. Should the thatch become too waterlogged, the hogs have to make for higher ground in the foothills, and in some of these areas they have to run the gauntlet of going through some of the small cultivated areas belonging to the immigrants who, as far as the Assamese authorities are concerned, were not officially allowed to be there.

During one of our habitat investigations in the Rajagarh Forest Reserve, the Willis jeep that Pearson and I were being driven in became stuck in the loose, hot sand of an empty river bed, and we had to spend a considerable amount of time gathering stones from the shoreline and pieces of wood, to provide sufficient traction for the vehicle to extricate itself. During the course of such an exercise, Pearson pointed out some very recent pug marks of a tiger and that, as an ex-shikari himself, he could assure me that the possessor of such paws would represent a sizeable trophy. With some personal knowledge of how an adult African lioness likes to stalk its prey, I kept a very wary eye on the thicket on the north bank of the river bed, which had been the direction to which the spore had led, while at the same time speeding up my assistance in recovering the jeep in order to retire as quickly as possible from the vicinity of such a predator. If a hungry tiger had decided to retrace its footsteps and pay us a visit, apart from trying to squeeze under the vehicle, which hopefully would be much too small an aperture for a fully grown tiger to join one under, I was at a total loss to think of any other survival tactic that could be adopted, for we were totally unarmed.

It had been in the late 1960s and early 1970s that conservationists were studying the survival potential of the Indian tiger, for the prime ministers of India and Bangladesh, and the late king of Nepal, all expressed their intense interest in saving the tiger, which they regarded as part of their natural heritage. At this time, Guy Mountfort reported that all three governments were already actively co-operating with IUCN and the WWF. The tiger was adopted as the symbol of Bangladesh, whereas India had named it as their 'national animal', and Shrimati Gandhi had appealed to all the Indian States to improve the protection of the species. It was in 1970 that all three countries had passed legislation banning tiger-hunting and the export of skins.

In 1973 'Project Tiger' was launched by India with great fanfares to save the species from extinction, and, thanks to the initiative of Guy Mountfort, Arjan Singh, the Indian government, the IUCN and WWF, the project succeeded in reversing the decline of what has been termed as the greatest predator on earth. Since that time, sixteen special reserves have been declared and the population is said to have risen from 1,800 to more than 4,000 today. With an estimated population of 40,000 at the height of the British Raj, shikaris had long declared an open season on these most mighty of great cats. The Maharaja of Udaipur was reported to have accounted for 1,000, and as recently as 1939, a former viceroy of

An 'on site' captive breeding programme has been started for the world's rarest tortoise: the Angonoka or plowshare tortoise (David Curl)

India was reputed to have shot 120 during a ten-week expedition in the Chitawan Valley, Nepal.

A recent serious outbreak of man-eating in the north of India suggests to some conservationists that there are now too many tigers for the space available, so the question has been asked whether the rescue operation has been too successful. With the inexorable build-up of India's human population, increasing at 3 per cent a year to a total that has now passed 800 billion, people are drawn closer to the protected areas by the search for farmland, as well as by the fact that anyone living within 5km (3 miles) of a park boundary has a traditional right to cut forage, firewood and thatching materials in the forest.

Arjan Singh, still one of the tiger's staunchest friends, has recently called for the creation of buffer-zones around the Dudhwa National Park, near to his home in Uttar-Pradesh. In these zones, only crops like wheat or barley will be grown, so that tigers will not lie in them to await their prey; in this way, he believes, men and tigers could keep apart and co-exist without the present friction. He has also called for the splitting up of the Forest Department into two, establishing a separate conservation branch. Undoubtedly, 4,000 tigers require a great deal of space, so it is now well recognised that the future management of these big cats presents conservationists with one of the greatest challenges they have had to face to date.

On one occasion, I had the opportunity to ride on one of the Forest Department's elephants through the tall grass, and recalled an account of the pigmy hogs' lively but tenacious disposition that was recorded by Lord Frederic

131

Hamilton in his book *Here, There and Everywhere*, which describes a shooting party with the Maharajah of Cooch Behar in 1891. He stated:

They go about in droves of about fifty and move through the grass with such rapidity that the eye is unable to follow them. The elephants, oddly enough, are scared to death of the pigmy hogs, for the little creatures have tusks as sharp as razors and gash the elephant's feet with them as they rush past them.

Perhaps this was the only occasion when I was pleased that I was not in close proximity to such a population of tenacious miniature pigs, while I was mounted on my pachyderm bearer.

Although such events took place some eighty years prior to my visit to Assam, the life-style of, and attention to detail afforded the guests who participated in such shooting parties made some of the privations that I experienced on the Zaire River Expedition seem totally unnecessary. Lord Hamilton recorded that the Maharajah's private orchestra of thirty-five natives who played in an almost untrodden jungle under a skilled Viennese conductor was a startling incongruity. The shooting party's retainers numbered 473, including mahouts and elephant-tenders, grooms, armourers, taxidermists, tailors, shoemakers, a native doctor and a dispenser, boatmen, cooks, bakers and table-waiters. An excellent European repast was served on solid silver plates, with the endless resources of the camp including an ice-making machine so that iced champagne could be served each evening. Lord Hamilton recorded, as an example of how thorough the maharajah was in his arrangements, that he took three native gardeners with him, their sole function being to gather wild jungle-flowers daily and to decorate the tables and tents with them.

As Johnny Tessier-Yandell had told us, an entirely unexpected bonus, resulting from the reappearance of the pigmy hog, had been the incidental capture of a hispid hare. Although zoologists considered that the hispid hare probably still existed in a few isolated parts of their range in the grassy or scrub-like forest areas

132

along the foothills of the Himalayas in United Province, Bihar, West Bengal and Assam, it had not been recorded for some fifteen years, when a German zoological team had examined one that had been collected in the Goalpara Division of Assam in 1956.

In April 1971, Warendra Singh had acquired a male specimen of hispid hare that had fled from the Barnash Reserve Forest into his tea garden after the severe thatch fires a month earlier. When I examined the individual, it had lost its left hind leg and was, not surprisingly, of a very nervous disposition. The distinguishing characteristic of this species is its short and broad ears and small eyes. Its coat was most unusual, for, while the outer fur is coarse and bristly, the under fur is much shorter and finer. The coloration is dark brown and blackish, with numerous scattered, whitish bristly hairs; this colour shaded to a brownish-white on the underparts. I took the opportunity to take measurements so that I could add to the sparse data collected. The hare measured 45cm (18in) from nose-tip to end of tail, had a shoulder height of 18cm (7in) and an ear and tail length of 5cm (2¼in) and 13cm (½in) respectively. Because it had lost a leg, I saw no point in putting it through the stress of being placed in a bag in order to record its weight. Although this species was reputed to be somewhat unhare-like and to live in burrows, there had been no signs of this particular specimen doing so, nor digging, nor even scraping on the earthen floor of its accommodation.

After I had completed the majority of my observations on the captive population of pigmy hogs, one of the Williamson Magor Company's single-engine Cessna 180s flew Pearson and myself along the foothills to the east of the Mangaldai sub-division, over and along some of the lesser riverines of the Brahmaputra to north Lakhimpur, Dibrugarh, as far to the north-east as the region of Sadiya. The foothill savannah belt was lightly forested and appeared to be some 8–24km (5–15 miles) in width, and looked in places to be comparatively

The hispid hare was thought extinct until its joint rediscovery with the sympatric pigmy hog in Northern Assam in 1971 (Diana Bell)

A fine stand of tea at Borengajuli, Assam, near to the heart of pigmy hog country

discontinuous. It was in these regions that it was only too evident how dramatic the transformation of the previous 'wilderness' had been by the progressive settlement of the immigrants that had resulted in the replacement of practically all natural habitat, up to the boundaries of forest reserves.

From gaining a bird's-eye view of the pigmy hogs' remaining habitat, it was very easy to understand how such pressure on their homelands, sandwiched as they were between the tea gardens to the south and the Himalayas to the north, by the illegal immigrants from Nepal, about whom the Assamese authorities were not prepared to do anything at this particular time, was steadily eroding it. Perhaps the Chinese armies' saunter into Assam in the early 1960s would have been determined that much earlier had there been some human settlements within these border regions that could have raised the alarm.

The flight along the border regions between Assam and the north-east frontier area was perhaps the most dramatic that I had experienced, on account of the sensation of flying in a four-seater aircraft among the monsoon clouds, one minute having everything shrouded in front of the fuselage, then the clouds drawing apart like curtains on a stage to reveal sun-drenched peaks, paddy fields and the magic of such enchanted frontier regions. On returning once more to the west towards Bhutan, we touched down at Harthura and lunched with the Williamson Magor Company's senior executive in Assam, John Oliver, at his attractive double-storey tea-planter's house.

After lunch, the Cessna flew Pearson and me to Gauhati in time for us to catch a scheduled passenger flight to Behora, for it was from the Behora Tea Estate that I was to be given the opportunity of visiting the famous Kaziranga Wildlife Sanctuary.

Our host at Behora was Ian Walker, an ex-wartime Royal Naval Officer who had come to Assam in the late 1940s and who had rejoiced in the solace of such a picturesque environment ever since. The following day, after a luncheon at the Jorhat Club, some 56km (35 miles) to the east of Behora, we were collected by a well-known Indian conservationist, Dr Robin Banerjee: Since the death of E.P. Gee, author of the classic work on the wildlife of India and after whom the golden langur had been named, Robin Banerjee at that stage had done perhaps more than anyone else to further the cause of conservation in Assam. The illustrated talks that he had given to schools throughout the state had helped to provide the children with an awareness as to the importance of their wildlife heritage. On lecture tours in Europe, from his interviews on television and on the radio, and through his wildlife films about the occupants of Kaziranga, he had

The Asiatic lion is restricted to the Gir forest that lies within the State of Junagadh, in the north-western corner of India, where it is listed as an endangered species (Phillip Coffey)

raised money to help in the fight against poachers as well as helping to sustain the proper policing of the wildlife sanctuary.

We arrived at the rest house at Kaziranga, which is situated just outside the sanctuary, just after 4pm when the cool of the day had already replenished some of our sagging energy. The sanctuary stretches for some 40km (25 miles) along the southern bank of the Brahmaputra, just to the north of the Mikir Hills in central Assam. The area was both a sportsman's and poacher's paradise until 1908, when it was realised by the authorities that, owing to the rapid rate of the disappearance of wildlife, steps would have to be taken if any animals were going to have a chance to survive in the Brahmaputra Valley. After initially being constituted as a forest reserve and closed to shooting, Kaziranga became a 'game sanctuary' in 1926. In the late 1940s, after India's independence, its name was officially altered to 'Wildlife Sanctuary'.

Robin had arranged for us to be collected by an elephant from just inside the sanctuary's gates at 4.40pm. We climbed up a wooden ladder onto the improvised mounting block, then clambered over onto the spacious back of the swaying elephant. I sat over the elephant's shoulders, Robin was in the middle and Pearson took up the rear station of the back. The mahout sat astride the neck and twitched a small length of cane in readiness for some two hours of jockeying the elephant around the sanctuary.

The mahout gave the signal, and the elephant prepared itself and ambled forward in a swaying gait, and before long it was taking us through the tall grass habitat that provides so many species with their life-line and ultimate sanctuary. The elephant barged its way through the thick thatch until eventually we came out of the dense vegetation onto the flat grassy terrain of the Brahmaputra alluvium. Within minutes of breaking cover, we came across the prehistoric form of a great Indian one-horned rhinoceros, which was three-quarters submerged in a particularly marshy region. Perched on its armour-plated back were two snowy-white cattle egrets enjoying a feast on the multiplicity of parasites to which the rhinoceros was playing host. The rhinoceros was obviously used to the presence of elephants festooned with human beings and remained stolidly unruffled. Its ears were plumed with tufts of rufous-brown hairs and pricked forward like a donkey's. Provided the elephant kept her distance and did not attempt to enter the water, the rhinoceros seemed to be content to continue wallowing and to act as a spectator.

During the course of the elephant ride around Kaziranga, we saw in excess of twenty rhinoceros, and a good percentage of these were accompanied by their young. The calves represented a miniature version of their seemingly armour-plated tank-like parents. In some cases, it was possible to get within a few yards of them, especially while traversing in and out of the tall grasses, whereon they would snort in apprehension and disapproval of the elephant's immediate presence, turning abruptly away from us to trot off a short distance before wheeling about to face the intruding elephant again. Because the rhinoceros has been habituated to the sanctuary's elephants in this way, they seldom made an attempt to charge; although in such an event happening, the elephants have been trained by their mahouts to stand their ground staunchly for, as E.P. Gee recorded, the one-horned rhino will very seldom press home its attack.

One bull rhinoceros had a large gouge in its left flank, an ugly wound measuring

22–30cm (9–12in) in diameter that appeared to have only recently happened. Such inflictions were normally the result of a duel for mating dominance, and the loser was now on his way to submerge his wound in the caressing muddy waters of a nearby 'wallow' in order to prevent the invasion of flies and other insects from laying their eggs in the crevices of such an inviting labyrinth of tissue. Drawing nearer to the river, we approached from down-wind a herd of Indian swamp deer while the last rays of the evening sun generated a rich glow over their red-brown coats and cast delicate shadows all about them. The hooves of these deer are similar to those of the sitatunga of Central Africa, being splayed out in order to provide them with greater support in soft ground – an adaptation for living in swampy environments. A further characteristic is that swamp deer have bachelor herds of twenty to thirty individuals who, for the majority of the year, remain together, until just prior to the breeding season, when the senior stags engage in pugilistic combat for the right to serve as many hinds as possible.

We caught a fleeting glimpse of a pair of hog deer which had been disturbed by our elephant's progress through the tall grass, the latter brushing our feet as we bulldozed our way through it. A small family group of Indian wild boar was taken fully by surprise when we suddenly came across them cooling off in a mud wallow. The patriarch emerged from the water, his large bulk festooned with weed, and stood threateningly between the elephant and his family. It was difficult to determine whether he considered that the weed was serving as a type of camouflage, but we decided not to encroach on his family further, so that at least he would appear to be victor.

Among the bird life of the sanctuary, lesser adjutant storks could be seen in different parts, prodding the rewarding earth for their daily rations of animal protein and vegetable matter. A flock of pelicans looked at us with all the suspicion of a group of black-market fishmongers, before electing to fly off to another stretch of water to continue with their late evening prunings and final meal of the day. A small cloud of ring-necked parakeets flew overhead, protesting at having been disturbed during their final feastings of the day.

In spite of the presence of the Bengal tiger, wild elephants, water buffalo, barking deer, and all the winged beauty of the wealth of animals that are to be found in Kaziranga, the concentration of the great Indian one-horned rhinoceros represents the pièce de résistance of the sanctuary.

The forestry department's policy, of showing more and more Indian school children around the sanctuary, and through the many educational talks that both the department and Robin Banerjee were providing the local schools with, had already greatly reduced some of the pressures on this, one of the last strongholds of India's wildlife heritage. The same evening, we returned to Robin's house at Golaghat and, after seeing some of his excellent animal conservation films, we talked into the early hours of the morning about further measures that could be adopted to secure, for the long term, the preservation of such a wealth of wildlife.

The following day, we were taken to the Moabund Tea Estate to meet Mr Wazir Khan, who considered himself to be one of the few people to have seen the pigmy hog in the wild. After proving to be a mine of information about both Assam's forest and animal life, he proudly displayed three pairs of elephant tusks and a tiger and a leopard skin, all of which had been taken from animals that he had been requested by the Forest Department to destroy because the specimens had encroached too much on the domain of the local population. However, it was obvious that, from our discussions, like so many former, and even present shikaris, he had a great respect for wildlife and was now an ardent conservationist.

My final few days in Assam were occupied with writing a comprehensive report on the various observations that had been made and recording the data that had been collected during my mission, as well as providing guidelines as to what I considered were important measures to be adopted to provide the optimum captive conditions for the pigmy hogs that were already held by the three tea estates concerned. Owing to the surprisingly tame disposition of the animals that I had examined and the successful reproduction that had already taken place in spite of the lack of privacy that had been afforded to the sow, I considered that there was every chance of a successful captive breeding programme for this species evolving from such a founder population. Having established a good management criteria and listed the types of observations that it was important always to record for us to glean as much as possible about the species' biology under captive conditions, I left Assam with a considerable amount of confidence that it would not be too long before a captive reservoir of this endangered species could be secured.

The Greatest Predator on Earth

The launch of Project Tiger by India in 1973 drew world attention to the critically endangered status of this greatest predator on earth. Project Tiger has succeeded in reversing the decline by the setting up of sixteen reserves and the tiger population is estimated to have risen from 1,800 to more than 4,000 today.

The tiger must surely take pride of place among Asia's large cats. However, until comparatively recently very few naturalists had studied this magnificent animal in the field except over the sights of a sporting rifle. A report from earlier on in the century of one man-eater credited with causing the destruction of thirteen villages and the desertion of over two hundred and fifty square miles of land, can see how man's relations with the tiger had previously been almost entirely on a kill or be killed basis.

Fiona and Mel Sunquist have recently carried out a two year field study of the elusive and highly endangered tigers within the tall grasslands and sal forests of the Royal Chitwan National Park, Nepal; and have monitored these solitary, nocturnal animals as they hunted, mated and raised cubs. The gathering of such detailed information on the tigers' personalities, food habits, living arrangements and interactions with each other and with other animals in the reserve – rhinos, leopards, sloth bears and deer, provide conservationists with an invaluable insight into how best the efforts to save tigers from extinction can be co-ordinated and arrived at.

Arjan Singh, who had advocated in 1972 that the tiger should become India's national animal, has subsequently played a leading role in the crusade to save this most impressive and powerful member of the Asiatic animal kingdom. Singh recently highlighted that in some regions there are now too many tigers for the space available, and that with the poaching of tiger-prey animals in protected areas, populations of deer and wild pig have been drastically reduced.

With India's human population estimated to be increasing at 3% a year, with the total now having passed 800 million, Arjan Singh's findings present a depressing long-term future for the ultimate chance of survival of the tiger species, for he relates: 'The combination of less prey, more people, and shared living space is a recipe for disaster'. Since the inception of Project Tiger, the strenuous international efforts carried out by the World Wildlife Fund to help the governments of countries, where tigers occur, to sustain the protected regions has undoubtedly proved to be invaluable; not only for the protection of the tiger species, but also for the continued survival of the thousand of other vertebrates and invertebrates that share their habitat with them.

While I was in Calcutta, I accepted it as my duty to give a twenty-minute feature interview on All India Radio as well as a three-minute news item concerning the significance of the pigmy hogs' reappearance in northern Assam. I took the opportunity to applaud the recent acceptance by Mrs Indira Gandhi of the invitation, from Richard Magor, to become Patron of the Assam Valley Wildlife Scheme, and underlined how such a dramatic reappearance of the pigmy hog represented a reprieve for a species that had been considered by some authorities to have already become extinct, and that it now provided conservationists with a seldom-offered second opportunity to establish a conservation strategy that would result in the preservation of this unique species for posterity.

Providing school children with the opportunity to witness the wildlife heritage of Kaziranga represents an invaluable experience that will aid the sanctuaries long term future

·10·

The Plight of the Pigmy Hog

SINCE the reappearance of the pigmy hog in 1971, and during the five-year period up to 1976, a considerable number of animals had fled from the increased amount of thatch fires that were systematically eroding the viability of the hogs' former habitat; some of these had taken refuge, either in the foothills of the Himalayas to the north, or in the tea gardens to the south. The majority of the escapees ended their lives in cooking pots or, as was the case for thirty-one specimens, had been rescued and maintained in captivity, either in tea gardens or at the Gauhati Zoo; from these, it had been hoped that viable breeding populations would materialise.

Although the pigmy hog had been afforded total protection under India's Wildlife Protection Act of 1972, the act did little to prevent the loss of the remaining habitat and known remnant populations of pigmy hog. The Indian conservationist, M.K. Ranjitsingh, had advocated that a suitable area of habitat should be fenced off, possibly in the Barnadi Forest Reserve, or in the Uchila central area of the Manas Sanctuary, so that the species could be protected, studied and a controlled breeding programme initiated.

During 1975, the Assam Valley Wildlife Scheme (AVWS), in collaboration with the Assam Forest Department, erected a chain-link fence round a 5ha (12 acre) enclosure in the Orang Wildlife Sanctuary. In the May of the following year, a pair of pigmy hogs were released by the Chairman of AVWS, John Oliver, into a small area within the enclosure; however, some two months later, they were reported to have escaped into the larger fenced-in area and no further sightings of them were recorded.

Ten pigmy hogs were born in three litters during the two years between 1973 and 1976, at two of the Williamson Magor Company Tea Estates and at the Gauhati Zoo. However, by the latter part of 1976, only seven of the thirty-one animals that had been rescued from the thatch fires still survived. It was evident from such disappointing results that a much greater degree of professional management and husbandry requirements would be necessary if such an unacceptably high degree of mortality was to be checked, and if the pigmy hog species was to be given a real chance to establish itself successfully in a scientifically managed site or sites.

It was in pursuance of such a conservation goal that, on behalf of the Jersey Wildlife Preservation Trust, Sir Peter Scott, the then Chairman of the Survival

Service Commission of the International Union for Conservation of Nature (IUCN) wrote to India's Prime Minister, Indira Gandhi, on 15 March 1976. Sir Peter stated that as these unusual animals were now being successfully bred in India, it would be of great biological and conservation value if a further breeding colony could be established in Europe, and that, as Gerald Durrell's Jersey Trust had been formed for the express purpose of building up breeding colonies of various threatened species, he was satisfied that it would be a most suitable place for such a project.

After several months, a reply from the Indian prime minister was finally sent to Sir Peter, which stated:

> In your letter of the 15th March, you asked for two or three pairs of Pigmy Hogs from Assam for the Jersey Wildlife Preservation Trust. This animal has reached the very edge of extinction but because of our strict protection, it is now making good recovery and we are able to spare some for breeding. I hope they will do well in Jersey.

Two days after this letter had arrived, I arrived in Bombay en route to collect the consignment of pigmy hogs. My visit to the city began with a trip to the Borivali National Park, which had only recently been given national park status, for its approximate area of 67sq km (26sq miles) represents the main water catchment area for the city of Bombay. In close proximity to the park's entrance was a compound that held between twenty-five to thirty chital, or spotted deer, which are perhaps the most beautiful of all Asia's deer family, their coats being a bright rufous-fawn, profusely spotted with white at all ages and in all seasons, although the older bucks are slightly brownish in colour and darker. The lower series of spots on the flanks are arranged in longitudinal rows and the graceful antlers have three tines. Mr Panday, a council member of the BNHS, told me that it was their hope to release some of the deer into the park so that further herds of chital could develop in the newly established sanctuary.

The lush vegetation of Borivali was in striking contrast to the spoliation of the landscape by the overcrowded population which surrounded and pressurised the park's boundaries. Such differences of environments that could be experienced in such a short period of time represented a dramatic reminder of how quickly man is able to render a given habitat into a state of impotency.

The most dramatic experience of this visit was the exploration of the interiors of the Kanheri caves, which contain a Buddhist temple and over one hundred excavated caves which play host to two species of bat: the fulvous fruit bat (*Rousettus leschenaulti*) and the bearded sheath-tailed bat (*Taphozous melanopogon*). The two bat species live entirely separate lives by inhabiting alternate caves. The interior of the first cave was very dank, probably some 20–25°F lower than the humid tropical temperature outside. Also, the stench of the thick carpet of faecal matter from the density of fulvous fruit bats was overpowering. Although trees usually provide the diurnal retreats for fruit bats, the *Rousette* is a habitual cave-dweller. On the whole, caves provide a great number of insectivorous bat species with the uniform conditions of temperature that they find the most suitable. The thick walls of caves and the high-domed architecture of excavated temples are much favoured by bats for, however high the

141

temperature of the air outside, it is cool within these retreats. Hundreds, and possibly thousands, of fruit bats were hanging within every crevice and from every ledge imaginable. The noise from their wings as they constantly flew to and fro and the lower frequency sounds the bats emitted in comparison with the insectivorous species, represented a barrage of audible sound as their wing-beats fanned the stale air of the cave's innermost sanctuary.

In the adjoining cave, the bearded sheath-tailed bats appeared to be in even greater profusion than the fruit bat species had been. With their long pointed wings, their speed and grace of movement, they compared favourably with flocks of swallows in the swiftest of flights. In sheath-tailed bats, the tail slips in and out of the membrane and helps to control the bat's movement and acts as a brake to flight; it may also be used as a large and capacious pouch for holding prey and an insect disabled by a blow of the wing is driven into this pouch, or cleverly netted as it falls in mid-air, before the bat thrusts its head into its pouch to kill its victim. The bat's highly developed echo apparatus represents a radar system of its own, enabling it to locate and evade even the minutest obstacle in its course. Although supersonic sounds emitted by them are constantly vibrating through the air which, after being deflected back, are instantly picked up by the bats, the bearded sheath-tailed bat, in addition to its high frequency sound, also produces a constant volume of 'chittering' or squeaking, sounds which effectively drowned any attempt on our part to talk to each other.

On our way out of Borivali, we startled an Indian peacock which flew up almost vertically in front of us and, in spite of its cumbrous 'tail' developed considerable speed, at the same time screaming its 'may-awe' calls in protest at being taken so much by surprise. What is not generally realised is that the gorgeous ocellated, or 'eyed', train of the cock bird is actually not its tail but abnormally lengthened upper tail-coverts. Just after we had seen a huge crocodile lying motionless, with its chin resting on the mud of the shallows, a Brahminy kite scooped up a fish from the surface of the water within a few feet of the crocodilian, but it was obviously astute enough to have just kept out of range of the fatal tail-lash of the motionless killer.

The following morning, Zafar Futehally had arranged for me to be interviewed on All India Radio and to discuss how the breeding of endangered species in captivity can act as an important insurance policy for a species' ultimate chance of survival. At midday, I was driven to the headquarters of the radio station where I presented a twenty-minute feature, followed by a three-to-four-minute news release interview which was to be copied and broadcast in New Delhi. I discussed the work of Gerald Durrell's Jersey Wildlife Preservation Trust, the joint Fauna Preservation Society and the JWPT's project with regard to the conservation of the pigmy hog, as well as the importance of Borivali and the additional support that should be given to the establishment of some more populations of the elegant chital within the park's boundaries.

In the afternoon, I met Asia's leading ornithologist, Dr Salim Ali, who had only comparatively recently co-authored a popular book with Laeeq Futehally on the common birds of India. Apart from his many research papers and other popular books, he was particularly known internationally for his nine-volume opus entitled the *Handbook of the Birds of India and Pakistan*, which he co-authored with the Secretary of the Smithsonian Institute, Washington DC, Dr Dillon Ripley. Salim possessed what is sometimes a rare ability among scientists to communicate his interest and enthusiasm to the layman.

On my arrival back at the Ritz Hotel, I found that a pay-slip had been sent to me in lieu of the morning's interview on All India Radio. As I was not an Indian national, was not a resident of the State of Bombay, and was on a visitor permit I was required to pay just in excess of 85 per cent of the standard fee for such broadcasts in tax. I was requested to sign the tax slip, as well as to advise where the balance should be paid; as I had just joined the BNHS, I signed over such a financial reward to the society although, because of its minimal size, recognising that it would hardly have underwritten a few pots of tea.

Early next morning, I was on the return journey to Calcutta where Pearson Surita welcomed me back. On this occasion, Pearson was not to accompany me to Assam but was arranging the many permits required for the pigmy hog exportation and the visa that was required for anyone entering Assam at that particular time, for, as the Indian National Congress Party had elected to have its annual conference in Assam that year, an embargo had been placed on all foreign tourists, preventing their entry until after the conference. Fortunately, because of the economic muscle of the Williamson Magor Company and the fact that I was in possession of a letter from Indira Gandhi, Pearson considered that I would be granted the necessary visa.

During the afternoon, I was provided with the opportunity to visit both India's National Library and the Calcutta Museum. It had been the Viceroy of India, Lord Curzon, who had first conceived the idea of opening a library to the general public but it was not until the turn of the century that it was officially opened by him. In 1953, the library was moved to its present location at Belvedere, once the home of Bengal's state governors. B.S. Kesavan was the chief librarian at the time of my visit and as soon as he realised that I was a book collector and shared his enthusiasm for antiquarian books and fine bindings, he escorted me through Belvedere's impressive main reading-room, down some stairs to a series of air-conditioned vaults which accommodated a wealth of illuminated manuscripts and lavishly embossed bindings – all the products of scribes and illuminators who sometimes worked on just one tome for years. Dr Kesavan provided me with a photocopy of B.H. Hodgson's 1847 paper that first described the pigmy hog and also presented me with an inscribed copy of his excellent illustrated publication on the history of India's National Library.

Dr B. Wiswas also gave up some of his precious time to show me around the mammal section of the Calcutta Museum. Various parts of the pigmy hog species were extracted from mothball-smelling cabinet drawers and display cases. Neither of the mounted specimens on display properly portrayed the correct stance of the pigmy hog, its hindquarters being shown lower as opposed to being higher than its head and shoulders. Perhaps, if the pigmy hog species had not 'reappeared' in 1971, mankind would have been permanently under a misconception regarding its stance. I took a series of notes regarding the nature and quantity of pigmy hog material that the museum possessed and promised to furnish Dr Wiswas with any further data on the pigmy hog that I considered would be of interest to the museum.

The following morning, Pearson accompanied me to the Calcutta offices of SAS, where the cargo sales representative listened patiently to my request to fly up to three pairs of pigmy hogs from Calcutta to Zurich on the 27 November. Owing to the stringent veterinary restrictions in force within the British Isles with regard to the importation of members of the pig family, it had been found necessary to find an alternative location to establish a captive breeding programme for them in Europe; and, because of the Jersey Trust's close links with breeding programmes at Zurich, we had arranged to have the animals quarantined and maintained at the Zurich Zoo. Once they had successfully reproduced, we knew that we would be granted the necessary permission to import European captive-bred stock to Jersey.

The majority of the next forty-eight hours was taken up by trying to secure the necessary export permits for up to three pairs of pigmy hog from India; my entry visa to Assam, and permission from Indian Airlines to convey the consignment with me from Gauhati to Calcutta. When the export permit did materialise from the Comptroller of Exports, it provided permission to export only two pairs of animals. So our messenger went back with the pigmy hog file, which included the official correspondence from both the prime minister and the Joint Secretary of Forests and Wildlife, Mr N.D. Jayal, both of whom had made mention of up to three pairs of the species.

Just when the latter exportation permit had been satisfactorily amended, I was visited by two sombre-looking officials, who required further copies of the New Delhi correspondence, which they told me was necessary for their office to present to the government of Assam. Perhaps the officials were from the state security, for they certainly appeared initially to examine the letters as if they were forgeries and they themselves were about to place me under arrest. No doubt there were now a number of senior officials in Calcutta attempting to fathom out what the hitherto unheard of pigmy hog of Assam was, and just why so much attention was being given to it by their prime minister.

Finally, however, all the official checking of my papers was over and I was in a position to fly to Gauhati to become acquainted with the pigmy hogs that I was to escort to Europe. On my arrival at Gauhati, I was met by Sayed Sayeedulla, the Williamson Magor Company's chief representative in that town, who had arranged a luncheon at his home so that I could meet Assam's Chief Conservator of Forests, Shri M.A. Islam, for it would be on his authority that the pigmy hogs would be allowed out of the territory.

The chief conservator of forests was most courteous and he soon informed me that he had read the paper setting out the data that I had collected about the pigmy hog, during my previous visit to his country, which had appeared in the journal of the Bombay Natural History Society in 1971. He thanked me for so generously and appropriately acknowledging the work of the Forest Department and the significance of the conservation measures they had adopted in Assam's national parks and wildlife sanctuaries and their contribution to the rehabilitation of endangered species such as the white-winged wood duck, the golden langur and the pigmy hog. Shri Islam then told me that he was in possession of the official documentation from New Delhi granting me permission to take six pigmy hogs out of Assam but that, regrettably, owing to the recent losses at the Gauhati Zoo, he could only allow me to remove one pair of this species from Assam at present.

I informed Shri Islam of my great disappointment at only being allowed to take just one pair of the pigmy hog and explained some of the inbreeding problems that manifest themselves when only one breeding pair is used as the founder stock. In spite of doing everything that I could to persuade the chief conservator to change his mind, he refused to be swayed, and I found myself in the unenviable position of realising that it was now too late for me to bale out of all the arrangements that had been made, for I considered that all the Indians with whom I had dealt to date would feel it a slight on their goodwill had I decided to refuse to take the one pair that I had been offered.

As if to console me for the disappointment over the pigmy hogs, I was taken, as Shri Islam's guest, to the Gauhati Zoo and the chief conservator proudly presented me with an inscribed copy of his booklet, *Our Forests and Forest Resources in Assam,* which had been published only some twenty-five days previously. The zoo was run by the Forest Department and had been established in 1957 at the time the Indian National Congress Party's last annual conference was held in Assam. Regrettably, it did not restrict itself either to Assamese or even Indian fauna, but exhibited such African animals as hippopotamus, chimpanzee and African lion, binturongs, as well as many species from the Indian sub-continent – large Indian civets, clouded leopards, and marbled cats, etc which were accommodated in somewhat depressing Victorian-type menagerie cages. In contrast, some attractive tall cages accommodated two family groups of the golden langur, which were basking in the mid-afternoon sun that enriched the longer hairs on their flanks to a deep golden-treacle-like complexion.

A pair of pigmy hogs, with their one surviving 1976-born young, kept running up and down the rear fence line of a large enclosure, which had been constructed through funds from the Williamson Magor Tea Company, via the Assam Valley Wildlife scheme. It was sad to see that the design had not taken into consideration the basic management and husbandry requirements that I had, in memorandum form, established during my first visit to Assam and which I had left with the authorities concerned, for without security and the ability to separate the adults just prior to and during the early part of the rearing process, it was unlikely that the facility could record the degree of success that should have been attainable. One factor I had not envisaged in my report was the frequent visitations of the endemic Indian mongoose into such a paddock and their stealing some of the hogs' daily rations. Also, one of that year's piglets had been predated upon by an eagle owl. It was evident that, unless the existing management regime was changed, the zoo would not be aiding the pigmy hogs' chances of survival. I therefore decided that, after my departure from Assam, I would write a tactful note to Shri Islam concerning the possible improvements that should be made in order to heighten the chances of the zoo recording more satisfactory results.

One large enclosure accommodated a breeding group of black buck, and on the thickly vegetated shoreline of a pond were a pair of sarus crane with two healthy-looking chicks. Adjacent to the pond was another water-fed paddock with an impressive Indian World Wildlife Fund education board about the endangered white-winged wood duck. The board read:

> This species of indigenous wild duck was considered to have disappeared completely from the face of the world. Some of the wild ducks of this species were recently discovered and a few of them captured alive . . . It is expected that by rearing this rare bird in captivity it will be possible to rehabilitate the same in its natural environment in Upper Assam and thus save the bird from total disappearance from the face of the world.

Although such phraseology could be regarded as quaint, I reflected what great strides had been made by zoos in recent years by providing their visitors with such an important awareness as to how imperative it was to conserve animal species, as well as how captive breeding could aid such measures.

The white-winged wood duck inhabits dense, primary tropical rain forest, close to slow-moving streams and sheltered pools. It was once widespread throughout most of the Indian sub-continent, but is now found only in a few scattered places in Assam, Bangladesh, Burma and possibly in Sumatra and Java. As a perching duck it spends the majority of its day under the umbrella of the rain forest trees and emerges to feed on the shallow marshes of swamp areas at dawn and dusk. Its ghostly wailing that echoes through the forest earned it the name of the 'spirit duck' among Assamese villagers.

The total wild population, throughout its former range, is now numbered in hundreds, and it was Sam Mackenzie, a tea planter in Assam, who had rediscovered the species and arranged for some to be sent to the headquarters of The Wildfowl Trust at Slimbridge. The Wildfowl Trust's extremely successful breeding programme has resulted in the establishment of a secure captive reservoir of this endangered species, and the Jersey Trust became one of the first centres to act as an extension to The Wildfowl Trust's captive breeding programme. To date, fifty-seven Jersey-bred white-winged wood ducks have been returned to The Wildfowl Trust at Arundel. These birds form a part of a strategy by The Wildfowl Trust to move this successful collaborative breeding programme into its third, and penultimate, phase for the re-establishment of the species in areas within its former range.

Swamp drainage and forest clearance have been given as the causes of the disappearance of the white-winged wood duck and it is to Thailand, where the

duck is no longer found in the wild, that the first captive-bred birds have been sent to establish a pre-release breeding nucleus before reintroduction within protected sanctuaries in that country is to be undertaken.

On our way over to the north bank of the Brahmaputra, Sayed told his driver to stop at the Indian Airline office, for I still had not received their approval to convey the pigmy hog consignment from Gauhati to Calcutta. In spite of Sayed gaining immediate access to the area manager's office, the manager was unable to provide us with the answer that we were waiting for, for he kept plaintively repeating that livestock of any form was not normally allowed on the Gauhati–Calcutta flight. However, after exerting as much moral pressure on him as possible, and underlining the importance and significance of his airline conveying

The Chital is perhaps the most beautiful of all deer with its bright rufous-fawn profusely spotted coat and is at its best in the Himalayan foothills (William Oliver)

such stock that has so significantly gained the attention of the sub-continent's prime minister and other overlords, he promised to request from his head office a special dispensation for such an important cargo.

I spent most of the following day at the Attareekhat tea garden, for it was from there that the solitary pair of pigmy hogs that Shri Islam was allowing me to take with me out of Assam, were accommodated. My first task was to organise the best way, when the time came, to catch up the two animals so that they could be crated for their long journey to Europe, for it was obviously of the utmost importance to minimise the amount of stress that such a timorous species would experience if they were subjected to any degree of panic before the usual traumas of travel. Owing to such a consideration, I had already decided that to net them would be highly counter-productive and had, therefore, elected to have a 'catch-up' crate made especially for such a purpose.

I reminded myself of the two almost inseparable serval cats that I had had in a disused tobacco barn in Rhodesia some fifteen years previously, prior to catching them up separately before flying them back to the British Isles. Adopting a similar strategy, I requested the Attareekhat tea-garden carpenter to dismantle six tea-chests and reassemble them in such a way that they formed one long crate, with solid plywood sides and floor, with a drop-slide at either end. The roof was to have a series of 5 x 5cm (2 x 2in) wooden slats with 2cm (1in) gaps between each, which would allow the insertion of a third drop-slide. The philosophy behind such a design was to enable the crate to be placed up against the perimeter of the area where the animals felt the most secure and, as was the case with the servals, become sufficiently satisfied with its presence so that they would adopt the 'catching-up' crate as their place of safety. However, I had found that, in order for the servals not to be put off by the alien smells of the outside world, it had been necessary to soil the crate with old bedding from the run, as well as to place further bedding over the top of the crate to form a thatch and afford additional privacy.

The catching-up crate was completed within the day and by the time that I was ready to return to Borengajuli, the crate had been placed at the rear within the pigmy hogs' run, the drop-slides removed, and it was almost completely covered by a mound of vegetation made up of a mixture of old bedding and freshly cut thatch. Just before retiring to bed that night, I received a telephone call informing me that the pigmy hogs had already taken up residency in their new abode.

The following week was taken up with trying to surmount the bureaucratic obstacles that kept presenting themselves. I was informed that I could not move the pigmy hogs from the Mangledai sub-division of the Darrang District of Assam to Gauhati without first acquiring a movement permit for the animals from the divisional forest officer. However, before such a movement permit would be granted, it would be necessary for me to possess a veterinary certificate stating that the animals were fit to travel, had not been exposed to any infectious disease and that swine fever had not occurred in the last two years within a 19km (12 mile) radius of where the animals were being held in captivity.

I contacted the local veterinary officer, Dr Misra, whom we arranged to collect and convey to Attareekhat so that he could see the animals for himself. When the pigmy hogs appeared from the refuge of the catch-up crate, it was obvious from the expression on Dr Misra's face that he found it difficult to understand why

Bats are the only mammal with wings and that are able to really fly. Fruit bats or 'flying foxes' are extremely gregarious, flying at about dusk to fruiting trees to feed (R.E. Stebbings)

these diminutive wild pigs were commanding such a great deal of attention. When I returned with him to be shown around the governmental experimental farm, of which he was in charge and which supported some one hundred and fifty domestic ducks, a motley collection of goats and a series of fish hatcheries and stocked ponds, he asked me seriously whether the chief objective of trying to establish a viable breeding programme for the pigmy hogs was in order to provide, in the most economic way, additional food protein for the occupants of the island of Jersey. It took me over an hour to convince him of the true objective of my mission.

Once the veterinary certificate was obtained, I was in a position to drive the three-hour journey to the office of the divisional forest officer. After thoroughly inspecting the entire contents of my pigmy hog file, the officer proceeded to consult large tomes of well-fingered governmental regulations relating to the movement of animal life from one region of India to another. At first, I had not realised that he had been searching for some previous movement of the pigmy hog species, until after about half an hour of sitting patiently and watching him turning the pages over and over, he informed me that the pigmy hog was not listed so that he was at a complete loss to know how he could authorise the movement of an animal that was not represented in his official directory. When I told him that, to the best of my knowledge, the pigmy hog species had only once previously been taken out of its home range and that had been during the early part of the 1880s when a quartet had been taken to the Zoological Society of London, he relaxed and wrote out the required transit permits.

With only four days to go prior to my scheduled departure time on the SAS flight from Calcutta to Zurich, Indian Airlines had still not confirmed whether they would fly the pigmy hogs down to Calcutta. Sayed, who by that time had returned to Gauhati, was pulling every string possible until, at the eleventh hour, the dispensation was granted, although the telex stated that the animals would have to be confined to crates and would not be allowed loose on the plane.

With the tailor-made travelling crates in full readiness for the journey, the pigmy hogs well habituated to the interior of the catching-up crate, although they were yet to be confined to it, and with all the required documentation in hand, I spent my penultimate day in Assam by taking a trip through the terai and over the border into Bhutan. Some weather-worn engravings and writing on a large boulder by the side of the dirt track signified the fact that we had crossed the international boundary between Assam and the kingdom of Bhutan.

As the thatchland gave way to the Himalayan foothills, we came across a group of working elephants, owned by the forestry department, that were tethered by ropes around one of their back legs; their mahouts were placing mounds of fodder in front of their wards, before settling themselves down

Will the Pigmy Hog gain a third reprieve?

The pigmy hog was first described by B. H. Hodgson in 1847. Due to the scarcity of reports during the intervening years, and the fact that the animal had remained virtually unstudied in the wild state, apart from some references to a few individuals held in captivity at the latter part of the last century, little had been recorded about the species by the end of the 1960s.

The dramatic 're-discovery' of the pigmy hog in the Himalayan foothills of Assam during March, 1971, put paid to various gathering reports that this interesting and unusual member of the pig family was feared to be extinct.

Apart from a pair of pigmy hog that were taken by the author, on a breeding loan agreement, from Assam to Zurich, Switzerland, in November 1976, the only previous individuals of this diminutive pig species to have been sent out of India had been almost a

hundred years previously, in 1882.

The first reproduction of the pigmy hog in captivity was recorded by the Zoological Society of London, after they had purchased one male and three females. Nine young were born at London Zoo during the period 1883–6, although none of these survived to adulthood. During the period 1971–9, some forty or so pigmy hogs were born in captive environments in Assam from a founder population of thirty-eight individuals. These births had occurred either at the Gauhati Zoo or from stock held at various tea gardens. Regrettably, in spite of the apparent ease of breeding from captive animals, due to poor standards of management the only pigmy hogs that remained in captivity by the end of 1979 were at the Gauhati Zoo and at Zurich. A litter of five (four male, one female) were born at Zurich Zoo

on 1 May 1977, but three months later the female died and by the end of 1983 none of the Zurich pigmy hogs were still living.

At the General Assembly of the IUCN, held in Madrid in November 1984, the pigmy hog was chosen as one of the twelve animals representing the world's most endangered species. Although it has full legal protection, there are many factors reducing its chances of survival and apart from the important population in the Manas Wildlife Sanctuary and its buffer reserve forests, the last decade or so has seen the pigmy hog exterminated from much of its former range. Unless appropriate habitat for this now critically endangered species can be sustained, the pigmy hog has little or no chance of making the twenty-first century.

for a mid-morning period of relaxation.

Before reaching the more luxuriant vegetation that is represented in the foothills, we passed an open-cast coal mine that had scarred an entire hillside with its terminal wounds that had now given rise to acute erosion. It was only possible to gauge the extent of such an operation by comparing the sizes of the ant-like work-force against the back-drop of such workings.

Butterflies and orchids abound in these frontier regions and there are purported to be over three hundred species of butterfly, and some one hundred species of orchid that grow on the branches of trees and on rocks, as well as on the ground. The ability of some species suddenly to announce themselves by conjuring up a beautiful flower from out of a branch of a tree, was as unexpected and as dramatic as coming across a large flock of colourful swallowtails feasting on some delectable material in the midday sun. The blue vanda and the bamboo orchid were both abundant in this foothill region and with the thickness of the deciduous trees, shrubs, climbers and other varied vegetation, such a scene engendered the type of environment that so aptly confirmed the exquisiteness of mother nature herself.

Just before we left Bhutan, a small party of the the yellow- and black-billed large pied hornbill flew from tree to tree in front of us, in their follow-my-leader characteristic style – a few rapid wing-strokes followed by a dipping glide, which culminated in a variety of raucous roars as they alighted on a large cluster of wild figs which they subsequently prodded with their outsize bills, then pecked at, tossed up in the air, caught and finally swallowed.

The following morning, I visited Attareekhat to provide the hogs with a feast of

The courtship display of a peacock with its gorgeous ocellated, or 'eyed', train that it arranges like a quivering fan, is a familiar sight for many (William Oliver)

their favourite foodstuffs, as well as to arrange the catching-up crate in such a way that they could be easily confined to it later in the day. As on almost all of the occasions that the animals had been seen to enter the crate, they had gone into it from the left-hand side, I decided to insert the right-end slide and leave it in the down position, at the same time leaving the left slide up in the drop position and inserting the slide in the roof, so that, once the animals were confined to the crate, the slide could be dropped in order to separate them. I watched the hogs finish their food and then, as if nothing had altered in their safe refuge, they returned to their former sanctuary.

As it was necessary to start my journey down to Gauhati at 5 o'clock the following morning, I decided to crate the animals just before sunset that evening and to take them to Borengajuli with me, where I could keep the two tailor-made travelling crates with the occupants in the adjoining bathroom of my room, and by doing so more ably monitor their welfare during this initial period of their confinement. Fortunately, on my return to Attareekhat, both the animals were still esconsed in the crate, sleeping off the effects of their mid-morning feast. I asked the Jotis to carrying on talking fairly loudly at the far end of the run, while I unbolted as silently as possible the door to the pen and, attempting to adopt the stealth of a cat, advanced on the crate until I was in a position to push down the left-end slide.

With this part of the exercise successfully accomplished, both of the travelling crates were brought into the run in readiness to place up against each end of the catching-up crate. However, before these could be put in place, I had to separate the hogs by dropping the slide in the roof and then establish through the slatted roof which end the male and female were. The travelling crates had been constructed to the IATA regulations' specifications for the pig species, although because these were mini pigs in comparison, I had reduced the advocated dimensions considerably. Also, I had arranged for the roof of each crate to be well padded, and the sides and the solid end, that was not a slide, to be well ventilated. Each crate had sufficient bedding in it to enable the hogs to gain as much security as possible. The male was the first to bolt through the lifted slides into its travelling crate and the female soon followed suit. We gently carried each crate and loaded it onto the back of the jeep with as much care as if we had been conveying a show-case of priceless Venetian glass and, escorted by the Joti's vehicle which went in advance of the jeep, we retraced our tracks to Borengajuli.

Apart from some minor grunts that seemed to be noises of reassurance to each other, the hogs appeared to have responded well to their respective changes of fortune. The crates were then deposited in my bathroom for the night. The following morning I decided that the strange noises connected with the running of a bath would cause the hogs too much stress, so I shaved in a small pool of water, after first providing each of my wards with one-and-a-half bananas, one tomato which I impregnated with some further moisture with the aid of a disposable syringe, and some oatmeal biscuits. At 5am the crates were taken to the jeep, where they were strapped tightly side by side in order to prevent any movement, and we had also taken the precaution of placing them upon an old mattress to cushion as many of the vibrations of the jeep travelling over the dirt road as possible.

As Gordon and Yfke (Simpson) were as anxious as I to ensure that the pigmy

hogs left Assam safely, they had insisted that they would both escort the jeep, in their car, on its journey to the airport, for not only did they want to help me through any bureaucratic obstacles with which I might be confronted but also, should something happen to the jeep on its journey south, at least their vehicle could act as a standby.

After an uneventful journey, during which I travelled with the jeep and its driver, we crossed over the muddy Brahmaputra three hours after having left Borengajuli, and arrived at the airport twenty minutes later. I checked both the hogs and they appeared to be in good fettle.

Although the flight was scheduled to take off at 9.30am, it was not until well after 10am that we were requested to bring the travelling crates to be weighed. With the male's crate weighing 30kg (66lb) and the female's 23.5 (52lb), I was charged 206.20 rupees for their passage to Calcutta. Two porters were hired to help secure a trolley for the crates, which was subsequently stationed in the shade. At 10.55, I gained permission to supervise the loading of the crates into the pressurised hold of the Boeing 737, and after the usual security checks, I bade a fond farewell to the Simpsons.

We touched down at Calcutta just after noon, where the temperature was 32°C (90°F). By the time that I had negotiated with an Indian Airline official for permission to go onto the tarmac and guide the hogs' unloading, the animals had already been taken to the freight department. The SAS representative informed me that the Zurich flight was scheduled to depart at 8.15pm and would be touching down at Karachi, Teheran, Athens, and arriving at Zurich just after noon Indian time (8am local time). I had requested to be allowed to inspect the hogs at each of the stops, but although this had been carefully considered by the SAS authorities, because of the recent spate of highjackings, such a dispensation – even for animal welfare reasons – was found to be impossible to grant.

The wild population of white-winged wood duck is numbered in only hundreds, a successful captive breeding programme by the Wildfowl Trust hopes to re-establish the species within areas of its former range (Phillip Coffey)

The crates had been left on a trolley, which has been wheeled into the coolest part of the Indian Airline's freight shed. At 3pm, I provided the hogs with their last major meal prior to the long flight to Europe and while I gingerly pushed the food through a small gap under each of their respective slides, the male stood up and champed his jaws in portrayal of his displeasure, while the female remained covered by a blanket of coarse wood-shavings, keeping secret the exact whereabout of her needle-like teeth. Considering the dramatic changes that had taken place to their daily routine during the last twenty-four hours, they had both travelled extremely well and were surprisingly calm.

Because of the nature of the official documentation that was accompanying the pigmy hogs, I was requested to present the file to the head of the airport customs. The prime minister's letter, the correspondence from the chief joint secretary in New Delhi, the well-decorated permits from Assam, all represented an impressive array which generated such a degree of curiosity that the custom's head decided that he would like to have a look at one of the animals for himself. So, after forty minutes of filling in further forms, the head officer accompanied me back to the freight shed. Both the hogs remained totally silent within their crates and it was obvious that the officer was becoming impatient at not being able to see one of the animals. Fortunately, I arranged a compromise by breaking up an oatmeal biscuit and pushing it through one of the ventilation holes into the male's crate. This action quickly mobilised the animal, which loudly snapped at the end of the crate through which the officer was looking. At first, the officer was quite startled, then regained his composure and courteously wished me good fortune with my ferocious-looking wards, seeming to be pleased with the fact that I was about to take them out of his country.

On Sunday 28 November 1976, Zurich was blanketed in snow when the plane touched down almost within seconds of the schedule time. Dr Christian Schmidt, of the Zurich Zoo, met me and immediately we headed for the cargo hold from which the hogs were about to be unloaded. With the temperature below zero, I was particularly worried about the hogs' welfare, but the transfer time from the hold to a heated van was kept to the minimum and although it took a further two hours to gain the necessary veterinary clearance before we left the airport, the inside of the vehicle was kept as warm as possible.

The hogs were to be quarantined in Zurich's old botanical garden building, where special accommodation had been made to receive them. Also, in order to satisfy Switzerland's stringent health requirements, a Gottingen miniature pig and a domestic bull calf were accommodated on either side of the hogs' pen to monitor any possible contagious disease. Just after noon, both the crates were placed against the rear of their well bedded-down quarantine quarters and the slides were raised so that the hogs could have access into more pleasant surroundings. Although there had been a certain amount of movement from the hogs while we had carried the crates, it was impossible to gauge their condition until they were completely clear of them. Fortunately, by 12.30, both the animals had emerged in a state of alertness, with no sign of them having suffered any shock, before they dashed for cover under a mound of hay.

The last pigmy hogs had been imported into Europe over ninety years earlier, when the Zoological Society of London had paid £125 for one male and three females. Although nine young were born between 1883 and 1886, none of these

Working elephant

were successfully reared. Now it was hoped that, with the help of modern zoo science – good accommodation, nutrition and veterinary care – Cal and Cutta (names that Christian Schmidt had immediately christened the pigmy hogs) would soon be recording a fruitful reproduction and successful rearings, for perhaps, if we proved the viability of such a collaborative conservation breeding programme, we would succeed in securing more hogs to enlarge the founder stock. In the meantime, however, we all recognised how much of a gamble we were sharing by having all the odds balanced so precariously on just one male and one female.

The breeding programme could not have got off to a more satisfactory start for, almost within five months of the hogs' arrival in Switzerland, they successfully gave birth on 1 May 1977 to four males and one female. Tragically, however, this fine start floundered, for although the four males were successfully reared, by the end of 1982 both Cal and Cutta had died and only three of the male siblings survived. Although attempts were made to have the remaining males breed with the domestic Gottingen miniature pig, these failed and by the end of 1984, no

155

further pigmy hogs were alive in Europe.

During 1984, William Oliver, research assistant at the Jersey Wildlife Preservation Trust, revisited Assam after a period of four years. Although, as a result of his previous pigmy hog field survey, he had presented a report to the appropriate national and forestry authorities concerned, calling for positive and effective action to be taken as a matter of urgency if the current rate of the pigmy hogs' decline was to be curtailed or even reduced, he found that nothing had been done to implement any of the recommended proposals for the conservation of this species. William found that, although the hog had full legal protection, its status had declined dramatically. The continuing encroachment of declared forest boundaries by immigrating settlers and the despoilment of virtually all remaining habitat in these areas, by dry-season burning, the harvesting of grass for roof thatch resulting in the deprivation of the hogs' cover and food, and it being hunted for meat, provided little hope for the species' chance of ultimate survival. Apart from an important population in the Manas Wildlife Sanctuary and its buffer reserve forests, since the species' reappearance in 1971, it has now been exterminated or at best made functionally extinct, from the majority of its former range in which it was known to occur.

At the IUCN General Assembly, held in Madrid in November 1984, the pigmy hog was chosen as one of the twelve animals representing the world's most endangered species. Gren Lucas, Chairman of IUCNs Species Survival Commission, declared that priority action was required to save the chosen representative threatened species from extinction, and he added: 'Although several are on the brink of extinction, we hope they will act as standard bearers to alert the world to the grave situation facing the complex web of life on earth for which we humans are responsible.'

Although it is recognised that there are still a great number of people in authoritative positions who are only interested in preserving wildlife if it has some obvious economic value, some of the authorities realise that the pigmy hog may represent a source of genetic stock for livestock breeding, which could benefit mankind. However, whatever the species' finer and more intrinsic attributes may prove to be, time for the pigmy hog is fast running out and it is doubtful that a third reprieve will be granted to prevent it from being categorised as 'possibly extinct', for even diminutive 'toy pigs' cannot be sustained without appropriate habitat, food supply and a secure life-style and, as with the dodo, extinction is forever.

Selected Bibliography

Publications by the author relating to the various species studied
during his travels in search of endangered species

South America

1966 'The River Turtles of the Amazon'
Oryx, Journal of Fauna Preservation Society Vol 8, No 4, p228; International
Turtle and Tortoise Society, Vol 1, No 1, pp34–5

1966 'Bolivia and the Vicuna'
Oryx, Journal of Fauna Preservation Society, Vol 8, No 5, p290

1984 'Lion Tamarins' Survival Hangs in Balance'
Oryx, Journal of Fauna and Flora Preservation Society, Vol 18 (2) pp72–8

1985 'The Plunder of the Golden Lion: Brazil's Endangered Primates'
Country Life, Vol CLXXVII, No 4565, pp368–9

1987 'International Efforts to Secure a Viable Population of the Golden-headed
Lion Tamarin'
IUCN/SSC Primate Newsletter: Primate Conservation No 8, pp124–5

Africa

1962 'Dangers Involved in the Exploitation of Game in N'Gamiland'
Oryx, Journal of Fauna Preservation Society, Vol 6, No 5, pp288–9

1963 'Wattled Crane in N'Gamiland'
Avicultural Magazine, Vol 69, No 3

1971 'The Modern Role of Zoological Institutions'
Rhodesia Science News, Vol 5, No 2, pp42–4

1973 *Okavango Adventure – In Search of Animals in Southern Africa*
(David & Charles)

1974 'Wildlife Studies on the Zaire River Expedition with Special Reference to
the Mountain Gorillas of Kahuzi-Biega'
Jersey Wildlife Preservation Trust Annual Report, Vol 11, pp16–23

1975 'Two Months in Zaire'
International Zoo News Magazine, Vol 22, No 127

1987 'Rhinos on the Brink'
Country Life, Vol CLXXXI, No 45, pp92–4

Madagascar

1970 'Madagascar – the Home of One of the Most Interesting and Scientifically
Valuable Faunas in the World'
Jersey Wildlife Preservation Trust Annual Report, Vol 7, pp62–7

1971 'The Lemur Collection at Parc Tsimbazaza'
International Zoo News Magazine, Vol 18, No 3, pp90–2

India
1971 'The Pigmy Hog *Sus salvanius* in Northern Assam'
Journal of Bombay Natural History Society, Vol 68, No 2, pp424–3
1971 'A Note on the Hispid Hare'
Journal of Bombay Natural History Society, Vol 68, No 2, pp443–4
1971 'Pigmy Hog and Hispid Hare'
Oryx, Journal of Fauna Preservation Society, Vol 11, pp2–3, 103–7
1971 'Breeding Animals in Zoological Gardens'
Concern for Man and his Environment Magazine, Bombay, India
1972 'A Visit to the Alipore Zoological Gardens, Calcutta'
International Zoo News Magazine Vol 19, No 2, pp42–3
1977 'Breeding of the Pigmy Hog in Northern Assam'
Journal of Bombay Natural History Society, Vol 74, No 2, pp288–98
1977 'The Re-discovery of the Pigmy Hog'
International Zoo News Magazine, Vol 24, No 6, pp17–20
1978 'International Co-operation for Captive Breeding of the Pigmy Hog'
International Zoo News Magazine, Vol 25, No 3, pp28–31
1986 'Plight of the Pigmy Hog'
Country Life, Vol CLXXIX, No 4635, pp1762–3

Miscellaneous
1980 'National and International Zoo Co-operation: An Example from the Jersey Wildlife Preservation Trust'
International Zoo Yearbook, Vol 20, pp179–80
1984 'Survival Reservoirs for Endangered Species: The Conservation Role of a Modern Zoo'
Biologist, Vol 31, No 2, pp79–84
1986 'The Importance of an Inter-disciplinary Approach: Getting the Conservation Act Together'
Primates, the Road to Self-Sustaining Populations, pp996–1003, ed by K. Benirschke (Springer-Verlag)
1988 'Conservation Role of a Modern Zoo: Why Zoos?'
UFAW *Courier,* No 24, pp15–26
1988 'Collaborative Conservation Efforts Carried Out by J.W.P.T. and Countries Containing Threatened Species'
International Zoo Yearbook, Vol 27, pp176–91

Index

Figures in *italics* refer to illustrations